Uncommon Women

JOAN KUFRIN

WITH PHOTOGRAPHS BY GEORGE KUFRIN

NEW CENTURY PUBLISHERS, INC.

Uncommon Women

Gwendolyn Brooks
Sarah Caldwell
Julie Harris
Mary McCarthy
Alice Neel
Roberta Peters
Maria Tallchief
Mary Lou Williams
Eugenia Zukerman

Printing Code
11   12   13   14   15   16

Library of Congress Cataloging in Publication Data

Kufrin, Joan.
    Uncommon women.

    1. Artists—United States—Biography.   2. Arts—
Modern—20th century—United States.   1. Title.
NX504.K8   700′ .92′ 2 [B] 81-11097
ISBN 0-8329-0109-1   AACR2

FOR EVE AND BEN

CONTENTS

PREFACE

This book seemed simple enough, when I began. The work of these nine artists had deeply touched my life, and I needed to talk about it with them.

For one thing, I was intensely curious about when they first *knew* they had to dance, to write, or paint. I wondered about the early choices they had made and who had encouraged them as children. What work had to be done, what disciplines did they master? That they had raw talent goes without saying; but how did they, out of all the talented people in the world, manage to channel their energies, their wills, to do the work they had chosen?

Were they ever discouraged in their pursuit of art—and what then? Did they ever give up, or want to? What sustained them when the rent had to be paid?

They are all women. How did they manage to have a family and children and still not relinquish their art?

When I wrote to the artists, I asked these same questions in my letters. I wasn't interested in their personal lives, and I told them that. I wanted only to talk about their work.

I originally planned to use the interview material in a book for young artists—young novelists, painters, musicians, poets, and actresses. It was to be a bridge of experience and thought from one generation of artists to another.

Doesn't that sound sedate, orderly, and cerebral? (I think I envisioned elegant hours of talk, with quiet wisdom emanating like incense.)

Little did I realize what a churning world of activity my husband, George, and I were entering. None of these artists, of course, was waiting around idly to be interviewed about her life's work. She was too busy working. The most difficult part of the entire project turned out to be finding time to talk. Not our time. Theirs. With schedules filled for months and even years, the interviews were tightly scheduled between or stolen from time allotted to other activities.

ix

That we asked for at least two sessions astonished them. They are used to giving brief, superficial interviews. They are not used to interviews that require delving back years into early memories, feelings, and motives.

Once an interview began, however, and the artist was certain we were there to discuss her work, time lost its importance. The ideas poured out; experiences not thought of in years were remembered and shared; books to read were found and offered; states of mind were expounded in splendid, unequivocal terms. Best of all, new ground was being broken. This was material I had not found in my research.

I learned quickly that these artists have no half-baked ideas. Why should they? They are at a point in their lives where they are sure and have nothing to lose. Consequently, there is no hesitation, no compromise in what they say. That does not mean they gave reckless answers. They answered even my most inane questions with thoughtful care and respect. I thank them for that.

We have heard a lot about why there are so few women artists: Male domination, historical attitudes, women's role as mothers—all these have kept women from creating art.

I learned another thing. These nine artists contradict all such reasoning. They show us that strength of will and belief in one's vision are what make an artist. No women's movement will ever do that.

I learned, too, that all these artists were frequently discouraged with their work, but none ever dreamed of giving up. When I broached that subject, I received frosty glares of indignation. With the exception of Mary McCarthy, whom I suspect was putting me on a bit, none was satisfied with what she had done. Always and always, they wanted to do it better next time.

Except for Gwendolyn Brooks, who laughed uproariously when I asked, all of them said they felt guilty about wasting time. She said, "I believe in enjoying life. Sometimes I just sit and *think*!"

For the seven artists who had children, motherhood was not easy, as you will see; yet none would have foregone it. I included information about a marriage only if it seemed apropos to the artist's work.

The book that finally emerges is more than a book for young artists. It speaks to all of us, whatever our age or sex and whether or not we are artists. What is says most urgently is that these nine did not hear the word "no." If they did, they ignored it and then tried another way. What they did heed was the music inside that had to be made, the words inside that had to be written, the images inside that had to be painted.

In short, they kept the appointments with themselves.

Joan Kufrin

ACKNOWLEDGMENTS

Special thanks must go to the following people for their help and encouragement on this book, above and beyond the call of duty and/or friendship.

First, to John Schroeder and Richard Faber of the Chicago Public Library, for their diligent and fruitful searches for seemingly non-existent research material. They found what I was looking for every time.

To William Baldwin, Jessie Hiller, Fredi Leaf, Sam Lyons and Ed Weiss for extensive, volunteer research on behalf of this book.

To Cassie and John Pyle and Lucy McIlvaine for their unending hospitality to us on our numerous trips to New York.

To Jessie Medenwald, who patiently transcribed the hours of interview tapes and who bore the brunt of the typing.

To Joy Hebert for the earliest enthusiasm and for golden advice.

And especially to George, who always understood what we were trying for, even when I forgot, and whose photographs made me remember.

And to Ben, who cheered me on when it was needed most.

Uncommon Women

1

THE DANCER

Maria Tallchief

Maria Tallchief is at the heart of this book.

Years before we met, I had been enthralled by her legendary role as the Firebird. I hadn't seen her dance it, but I exhausted the patience of a friend who had. She told me that Tallchief had seemed to fly; it was the most exquisite dancing she had ever seen, and tears came to her eyes when she thought about it, nearly thirty years later. If there was anything I wished my eyes had seen in their lifetime, it was Maria Tallchief dancing *Firebird*. I knew I never would.

But I often saw Maria Tallchief herself. She is a Chicagoan, as I am. Often I would hear her being interviewed before one of her many ballet productions for the Lyric Opera, and I was amused that the interviewers seemed to be in complete awe of her. It's no wonder. Maria Tallchief has an aura of utter self-control that somehow extends to those she's around.

In all of the interviews I watched and read, there was a lot of news about the ballets she was mounting and what was coming up, but there was never much personal information. Perhaps the interviewers were too inhibited to ask.

Even books about her failed to reveal much of the inner Tallchief—what made her dance, what disciplines she must have developed to achieve that superb mastery over her body. Later, I found that the writer who had written what is considered the official Tallchief biography had never even interviewed her subject!

When I thought about Maria Tallchief, other artists came to mind—poets, novelists, musicians, painters. I began to wonder not only how they managed to pursue their art but how they were able to harness and utilize their inner resources. It seems obvious that no matter how much raw talent a person may have, only strength of will will develop it; and in these days and times, strength of will does not seem to me to be much in our national character. That wondering became the nucleus of the book.

When I wrote to Maria, outlining my idea and asking if she would discuss with me the real work of the dancer, she was immediately enthusiastic. Though we never talked about it, I believe she was at a point in her life when she wanted to talk about what makes a dancer—and we both knew we weren't talking about ballet lessons.

So it began. Because she was then rehearsing at the Lyric Opera for her ballet in *Faust*, her time was limited. The longest time she could devote to an interview was fifteen minutes, so we had seven or eight interviews of fifteen minutes each. We talked over lunch. Hers was inevitably a hard-boiled egg and a cup of cottage cheese. Mine was considerably more substantial.

After we finished the chapter on the dancer, I did the eight additional chapters over the next year and a half. Much happened during that time to both of us. Her ballet school, which had been just a dream when I first interviewed her, became a reality. In 1980, when the Lyric Opera cut off funding for its ballet program, Maria was forced to find a new home for her dancers, but in doing so she was also able to establish a long-planned Chicago City Ballet School.

From my standpoint, I was looking at ballet in a different way. Our daughter Eve, who had never dreamed of dancing when I first interviewed Maria, was now enrolled at the Chicago Board of Education's Franklin Fine Arts Center and was studying dance. She enjoyed it so much and progressed so quickly that her teacher suggested formal ballet lessons in addition to her school classes. I was now looking at ballet from a mother's point of view.

It seemed these added dimensions ought to be part of one last interview with Maria Tallchief. It is added to the end of this chapter.

When she danced, critics groped for words to describe her.

"What can one say when faced with the closest to perfection that dancing mortals can achieve?" wrote one, helplessly.

"A diamond, strung on steel wire," tried another.

"She thrills the spirit, moves the heart, and brings to the eyes the tears that cannot be withheld, not only for the Swan Queen, but from the knowledge that this is a lovely and perfect thing," wrote another, and came close.

For over twenty years, Maria Tallchief enchanted audiences all over the world, dancing almost beyond the limits of her extraordinary powers, never content with a performance, wanting always to be "better and better and better."

First as a dancer with the Ballet Russe de Monte Carlo and later as prima ballerina with George Balanchine's New York City Ballet, she created breathtaking new performances as the nearly airborne Firebird and as the Snow Queen, the Sugarplum Fairy, the Swan Queen, the Fairy Gypsy, and in dozens of other roles.

In those glory days, ballet dominated her life.

It still does. Although Maria Tallchief gave up professional dancing thirteen years ago, she is today director of ballet for Chicago's Lyric Opera and produces a dozen ballets a year.

At fifty-five, her body and legs have the look and grace of a dancer twenty years younger. And she radiates that firmness of mind that only those with absolute mastery over their bodies can achieve. Nothing is wasted—movement, time, or breath. She walks fast, talks fast, eats fast!

But it's the face that rivets one's attention. Devoid of makeup, exquisite cheekbones lift attention immediately to the brown wide-set eyes that open wide or narrow dramatically with each sentence, each nuance.

In conjunction with the eyes and quite as expressive is an active brow. As Tallchief talks about ballet, young dancers, her own daughter, marriage, art, and regrets, her brow is constantly rising, wrinkling, frowning, or smoothing with her thoughts.

Later she would say to me, "I hate faces that have no questioning in them, no quest for wanting to learn more, look at more, see more, *be* more!" I understood that.

But now, within moments of our first meeting, Tallchief says unequivocally, "You cannot dance and leave it. When you make a commitment to ballet, it means *total* commitment. It doesn't mean going home and forgetting about it. You live ballet. You sleep ballet. Your whole life is that and nothing else.

"At night, when I wasn't dancing I would sew, and as I sewed I mentally reviewed everything that I had done during the day. I didn't even *read* during that time I was learning so much. I was afraid reading would break my concentration!

"And always I was practicing in front of the mirror. Remembering. Concentrating."

Concentration. Discipline. These subjects come up frequently in her conversation about young dancers.

"The sad thing," says Tallchief, shaking her head, "is the ones who have the most talent, the most beautiful figure, are *not* going to be the ones who make the grade. Why? Because they lack the concentration. The discipline. In my mind, they're one and the same thing.

"I don't remember that Balanchine had to tell me something more than once or twice. He would tell me something and I *lived* with it. When I say to the girls, you've got to point a toe this way and you can't do anything else, I'm not sure they go and live with that.

"You know," she adds, "I remember every correction Balanchine ever gave me. Or any correction that anybody else ever gave me! It becomes part of you.

"Visit our class. You'll *see* what I mean about concentration and discipline."

We arrive about 10:25 A.M. Five minutes before class begins. Twenty-eight dancers, ranging in age from sixteen to twenty-one, are on stage, warming up. It is quiet except for the sound of deep breathing as the girls coax, cajole, and stretch mortal flesh into impossible attitudes.

One girl lies flat on the floor. Her right leg slowly rises to a 90-degree angle, perpendicular to the floor. The leg continues on, widening the angle, and the leg slowly passes over the girl's shoulder. At rest, the leg is now flat on the floor above the girl's head!

Another dancer, bent double, knees locked in place, peers out from between her ankles.

A third, on her stomach, brings her feet to meet behind her head.

No fat to be seen here! No flab. Most of these girls have been dancing since age seven or eight and they are in excellent shape.

At thirteen or fourteen (some were lucky enough to be chosen at twelve), these girls were selected from competitions all over the country to receive Ford Foundation scholarships to the School of American Ballet in New York, which is the training school for both New York City Ballet and the American Ballet Theatre.

The point is clear: Ballet is a young girl's dream. It must be, if one's body is to be supple and limber enough to meet the enormous demands ballet will place upon it.

The dancers move to the barres, intent on the figure standing in front of them. Dressed in black jersey slacks and a black loose-fitting jersey jacket, Maria Tallchief surveys the dancers and indicates the tempo to the piano accompanist.

Ramrod straight, jeweled fingers on slender hips, head flung joyfully up and back, she walks among them as they do the barre exercises. With Tallchief, simple walking becomes a dance movement.

"Beautiful arches, please," comes the command.

A few beautiful arches are produced.

"Very nice, Jennifer."

But then, "This is a beautiful *moment*. Don't miss it! You really have to think about this step. It's hard to find, but it's there!" She taps her forehead.

"Think of your geometry. It's an arc, an arc, AN ARC!"

The exercises become more difficult. The barres are removed, and the girls dance *sur les pointes*.

"It's your body that dances, not just your feet," Tallchief cries. "Go to the Art Institute! Look at the Degas. See how the dancers *look*."

Over and over one hears the plea for beauty. For perfection.

"You must point the toe. Just so!"

This is elementary stuff, and it obviously irritates her to have to mention it.

"Beautiful arms, please. Beautiful feet. I explain it copiously, and I look over and you're doing *this*!"

Tallchief dissolves in a parody of wet noodles. The girls smile nervously (they never laugh aloud) and try again.

For an hour and a half they work. Always Maria Tallchief moves among them, smiling, sad, joyful, intent, frowning, and occasionally flashing a rare smile when she sees a beautiful step executed well.

"Yes, yes, yes, yes, YES!" she shouts, and one prays fervently that the girl will remember what she did to elicit such an exuberant "YES!"

At lunch afterwards, consuming a hard-boiled egg with obvious gusto, Maria smiles.

"I saw several beautiful things today. By that I mean the way a head looked, or a hand, or a sleekness of leg, or a beautiful line *en arabesque*. This, to me, is beautiful poetry. A beautiful piece of sculpture that one could gaze at forever."

But of course, in ballet one cannot gaze at the dancers forever. Unlike music, which can be played over and over again on records for a particular favorite passage, or literature, which can be read and reread, ballet offers only fleeting moments of beauty that vanish as they are happening. Maybe that is why this art form is so loved by its devoted followers. They know that what they are seeing will never happen in exactly this way again.

For Maria Tallchief, perfection was to be sought again and again and again. It was in the seeking that her art was formed.

"I remember my partner André Eglevsky once said to me, 'You know, Maria, you are never satisfied!' I said, 'I'm really not, André. I always feel I can do better than I've done.' And then I remember thinking if I were satisfied, then I would probably stop dancing because then, it's no longer interesting. Imagine. Just going through life being satisfied. It's not enough," she cries, her brow arrested in high position.

"Perfection. It is unfortunate for ballet dancers but it's there one day and perhaps it never comes again. I've seen it happen. On the other hand, with the true artist it becomes even better. Those are the ones who go on to become the great performers."

I ask about the elusive quality that differentiates a dancer from an artist.

"It's an ease and a serenity of performance. That's the difference. When you can see the effort that goes into it, if *that* is visible on the stage, that person isn't an artist.

"As Saint Exupéry said, 'Perfection is reached not when there is nothing more to add, but when there is nothing more to take away!'"

The hard-boiled egg and cheese are gone.

"Time has sped by," she cries, and then she too, disappears.

Another day, Elise Paschen, Maria's twenty-one year old daughter, joins us for lunch. We note that she orders a good substantial cheeseburger.

Elise, a vibrant blonde, is the only child of Maria and Henry (Buzzy) Paschen, Jr., the Chicago businessman whom Maria married twenty-five years ago.

Elise is preparing for a much anticipated trip to China with a friend. Ballet is forgotten for the time being as we talk about China, Harvard University (where Elise is a student), and the difficulties of a career in writing (which Elise is thinking about.) Above all, we talk about the China trip. Maria is preoccupied with details of shopping and packing, reminding Elise of things to be done. Later, after she has left, I ask Maria how it was to be a dancer and a mother.

A long look and Tallchief shakes her head.

"Very difficult."

When Elise was young, Maria took her along on tours and even tutored her. But that did not work out for long. Eventually, Elise had to stay in Chicago and begin school. Then the difficult times began. Maria found herself globetrotting, but alone. Her husband and daughter were back home. Though she was dancing and at the height of her career, "making more money than I ever thought possible," it was not enough.

"You cannot be a mother and dance," she says emphatically. "My emotions finally said, 'Alright, this is it.'"

So in 1966, Maria Tallchief stopped dancing professionally. She came home to Chicago to be with her daughter and her husband.

"I realize now I was still very young to give up ballet. I was only forty. But frankly, I had no other choice. Once you are torn between dancing and family, then you have to give up the dancing. It was time to stop. I never regretted it."

There is silence. She repeats, "Never," but not with the assurance of one who is completely convinced. Then she is gone.

The next time we meet, we continue our discussion of the past. Are there any regrets? In a career so filled with triumph and achievement, would she have done anything different had she known better?

The brow wrinkles in memory. The eyes dream. Yes, there was a major mistake.

Maria Tallchief's relationship with choreographer and head of the New York City Ballet George Balanchine has been a long and extremely close one. Balanchine, acknowledged universally as a genius and as America's foremost figure in the dance world, raised classical ballet to a new purity. Maria Tallchief was, at eighteen, his protegé, then his wife for nearly five years, and later the prima ballerina in his company. It is no secret that Balanchine created the Maria Tallchief the world remembers.

He not only created new ballets especially for her unique talents; but most important, he was responsible for the very technique that enabled her to dance his difficult works. When she met Balanchine, Maria Tallchief "saw and finally understood the fantastic legs and feet that were required of a classical ballerina." Under Balanchine's demanding supervision, the way her body looked literally changed. It took two years.

"Frankly, my whole physical being had to be made over again. My whole leg was pulled up and made long. The arches. The turnouts. All were changed."

Says Tallchief simply, "The man is a genius. His musicality, his timing, his response to music—all of this he puts into the human body. It is as though one is seeing nature at work. He was—and is—incredible to work with."

And exceedingly difficult. Take the *entrechat huit* business, for example. In this step, the dancer jumps and rapidly crosses the legs before and behind each other while in the air. *Entrechat huit* means that each leg makes four distinct crossings—eight movements in all! It is a most difficult feat, one that few dancers can bring off. Tallchief mastered the difficult step in several weeks.

"I learned it because Balanchine asked me to. It was what I felt he wanted. I doubt I would have learned it, if he hadn't asked. But you see, he asked." Tallchief never thought of not learning a step that seemed impossible. It only took longer.

The brown eyes drift away in reverie, remembering the effort.

The mistake, Maria? The regret?

Ah yes. She returns to the subject. The mistake came years after her divorce from Balanchine, a divorce she says was caused not by too much ballet in their lives, but by their tremendous age difference (she was twenty, he forty-two). Tallchief admits, too, of the strain of dancing as Mrs. Balanchine.

"I don't think George ever felt that, but I did. The pressure I felt because everything I did reflected on him. And I felt a great frustration that I wasn't better. I wanted to be better, and better, and better."

Still, even after the divorce, Maria Tallchief remained in the New York City Ballet as prima ballerina. Then, in 1954, she was offered "an unheard of amount of money for those days" to go on tour as guest artist with her former company, the Ballet Russe de Monte Carlo. She would be gone from the New York City Ballet for a year.

That was the mistake.

"At the time, nobody said to me, 'Oh, you mustn't go.' Had Balanchine just said to me, 'Why do you want to go? You're just now at your peak of dancing!' But he would never communicate like that at the time. And I shouldn't have gone. It was a mistake."

Why? Because, she realizes now, as director of a ballet company herself, when one is working with a dancer, as Balanchine was working with her, the director has hopes and plans and ideas for that dancer's development. For the dancer to abruptly leave for a year makes it extremely difficult for the ballet master.

"So, though I was offered a great amount of money—I had never heard of such a salary, nor had any other ballet dancer for that matter—still, what does that mean later? I wasn't any richer, or happier, or anything!"

Her voice trails off, thinking. Remembering. She shakes her head.

"I must fly. Time has sped by again."

And once more she vanishes.

Another day she is downcast. Frustrated.

"Ballet is like a football team. *Worse*. At least there one has a second string to fill in when injuries occur."

Four of her dancers have hurt themselves. One of them, the "best of the lot," will be out for two weeks at this critical time in rehearsal. She had sprained her ankle doing a step that is the very essence of this ballet. To Maria's practiced eye and touch, the ankle will require two weeks' rest. But then, she adds in resignation, pain and injuries are *always* present in ballet. Always.

"And if ballet is something you want to do, with ballet comes injury. Also exhaustion. Physical pain is the norm. It is what you expect.

"You mustn't feel that you are suffering if you can't eat. I used to go to bed hungry. Literally starving. Because I knew if I had eaten too much the day before, my body would not look right. I knew how I had to look on stage."

Hunger. Pain. Exhaustion. We painfully repeat these less-than-attractive facets of ballet.

She laughs.

"Oh, but one mustn't *think* about that! The pluses so outweigh the minuses.

It's just like having a baby. If given the chance you wouldn't say, 'Oh, I'd never do that again' just because of the pain, would you? It's the same with a dancer.

"We must command ourselves. This is where the discipline comes in. At 7:00 P.M. on the night of September 22, I am going to be on that stage, and I am going to give the best performance that I know how to give. Maybe I don't feel so well on September 22. Never mind!"

Where did you get that discipline, that ability to command your body to do your will?

"My mother," comes the instant reply. "I would never have been a dancer had it not been for her. She introduced me to ballet, but more important, she instilled in me the self-discipline that enabled me to concentrate."

A remarkable woman by any standards, Ruth Porter, a Kansan by birth, of Scottish, Irish, and Dutch ancestry, married Alexander Tall Chief, a well-to-do Osage Indian from Oklahoma. Tall Chief's money had come from oil discovered on the Osage reservation.

"My mother saw what happened to the rich Indians who dissipated their wealth through alcohol and lack of purpose in their lives. She was determined that her children not be allowed to go through life without discipline. She never planned for me to go into ballet as a career. She did want to give me and my sister the best exposure to art ... but the important thing was the discipline."

In today's light, the discipline seems almost harsh. Maria studied both piano and ballet. As a young girl of twelve, she would rise at 6:30, make her own breakfast, and practice piano from 7:00 to 8:00. Her mother would drive her to school and then pick her up afterwards. From 3:30 to 4:30, piano practice again, and then she would be driven to her dancing lesson, which lasted from 5:00 to 6:30. After dinner, homework and bed.

When the opportunities for studying the arts became too limited in Fairfax, Oklahoma, where the Tallchiefs lived, Ruth Porter Tallchief moved the family, with her husband's good-natured compliance, to Los Angeles. There, Maria (then Betty Marie) and her sister Marjorie studied first with Ernest Belcher, whose daughter Marge later danced with her husband Gower Champion.

When Maria was twelve, the sisters began serious study with Madame Nijinska, sister of the famed Russian dancer and choreographer Nijinsky. Madame Nijinska herself had trained and danced at the Maryinsky Theatre in St. Petersburg and had choreographed for the famed Diaghilev company.

Nijinska introduced Maria Tallchief to the world of the professional dancer. She took Maria to ballets and afterwards introduced her to the dancers.

"She paid a great deal of attention to me in class. But she never *said* anything. Nor did her husband ever come to my mother and say, 'Your daughter is very talented.' But just by the way she paid a great deal of attention to me in class, I felt that she was watching me constantly to see if I was doing what she wanted."

It became clear that Maria was doing exactly what Madame Nijinska wanted, when she gave Maria the coveted lead in her new ballet, *Chopin Concerto*. At the Hollywood Bowl premiere, Maria danced with sister Marjorie and Cyd Charisse.

Nijinska's ballet was to be even more important than Maria realized. A few years later, she danced her way out of the Ballet Russe corps de ballet forever when she was able to take over the same role for the injured ballerina, Krassovska. Then Krassovska left the company for good, and the *Chopin Concerto* role became hers just before the ballet premiered in New York. By such golden threads do careers sometimes hang. In *Chopin Concerto* critics for the first time really took notice of the "beautiful, dancing Osage." They predicted she was a young ballerina to watch.

There were many triumphs to come for Maria Tallchief: *Les Sylphides*, *Baiser de la Fée*, Eurydice in *Orpheus*, the Black Swan, the Sugar Plum Fairy, and of course, *Firebird*, a role with which she would forever be linked.

"I loved *Firebird*. It *was* my favorite. Except it was *terribly* difficult, physically. But once I finished with the first variation at the entrance, then I could relax and enjoy the rest of it.

"I'll tell you something, though. I never fantasized what I would be dancing in the future. Never. Never. NEVER. A dancer doesn't think like that.

"I only know that when I met Nijinska, I made the commitment to the pursuit of excellence in ballet. To me, she *was* ballet."

Maria never mentioned her decision to Nijinska. She never told her mother. But in her heart she knew she would be a dancer. She was twelve years old.

"You see, nobody can tell you anything if you want to do something desperately. And there was no way I wasn't going to dance!"

And, again, she is gone.

March 1981.

It's been nearly two years since I've seen her, but if anything, she looks younger and more vibrant than ever.

Her new studios occupy the top floor of a renovated loft building on Erie Street. Unlike the gloomy Civic Opera building that previously housed her company, here daylight pours into studios and offices through large windows on three sides, illuminating already white floors and walls.

And as usual, Maria has about fifteen minutes to talk. She has finished teaching one class; another will start shortly.

As we sit down, I tell her I'm spending a lot of time these days at the dance studio. Eve is studying ballet. Maria is delighted.

What am I going to tell her when she announces she wants to be a dancer, Maria, knowing what lies ahead?

"Nobody told *me* anything," she says.

Do you wish they had?

"No. I wanted to dance and I didn't want anything else. Time will tell with Eve. If the ingredients are there, she'll dance. But even if she never goes on the stage, ballet is something that will be with her forever. You know, young girls *love* the ballet. They just *know* they are becoming more beautiful as they work." She preens the way I've seen Eve do in front of the mirror. "You know, Elise studied ballet, and though she isn't a dancer, just the way she holds herself is beautiful."

I ask how things are going with her new Chicago City Ballet.

"Fantastic!" Her new company has a repertoire of nearly twenty works; they are dancing all over the Midwest. Auditions for the new school are always jammed. Enrollment in the school is near capacity; seventy children from the ages of eight through seventeen from the Chicago area make the twice-and sometimes thrice-weekly trip downtown for classes.

The school is modeled after George Balanchine's School of American Ballet in New York and uses his auditions and syllabi. It's the first time Balanchine has allowed that. His theory of teaching—and Maria's—is to start the child early.

"You take eight year olds, you train them for seven years, and at fifteen they're ready to go into the company. I had *always* thought about the school, but they wouldn't allow us to have one at the Opera House. I should have had a school six or seven years ago and would have had a complete company by now."

"It was a mixed blessing, then, that the opera company was forced to cut the funds for the ballet? It forced you to make the move?"

"What was I going to do? Here I had a company of trained dancers. I just couldn't let them go! When the Lyric could no longer afford a ballet company, Buzzy had just bought this building, and he said, 'Well, what about the building?' And I came and looked at it and saw that though there were large pillars, I was told they could be removed. So, here we are." She smiles.

"You make it sound very easy."

"It wasn't easy. It was very difficult!" She is astonished at such simplicity of mind.

"The problem, of course, is money. You have to *raise* it." The eyebrows soar. In the beginning she established a forty-four member board of directors from her well-heeled connections at the Lyric Opera for the new school; then she brought in Joseph Krakora, former vice-president of finance for the Joffrey Ballet, to manage the company. That helped. So did a $100,000 grant from the Illinois Arts Council, made under unprecedented prodding from the Illinois Legislature. But fund raising is—and will continue to be—an ongoing concern.

Finding good teachers is another. One of her best is pregnant, but has promised to return when the baby is a couple of months old.

And finally there is a matter of defection. Three dancers left last summer to join the New York City Ballet. But what could she say when they left? She did the same thing when she was young—went to New York. Maria obviously hopes that with the quality of her company and the repertoire, dancers will want to come here to Chicago and stay here. (The signs are promising. After only a year, in its new home, the company now numbers 26 and is growing.)

I have seen her in class and know that she is not effusive with compliments. I ask her about encouraging her dancers. Is there a fine line between too much encouragement and too little?

"Well, one has to be encouraged. *I* was encouraged by Madame Nijinska first, and then by Balanchine, but I believe in encouraging people mainly not through words, but by giving them the kind of roles to dance which are a challenge to them. That's the way we do it."

Her company is dancing primarily Balanchine works, though there are several by young choreographers. I ask if she does anything differently, now that she's teaching Balanchine's roles, than when she was dancing them.

"*No!* I remember what was told me by Balanchine, mainly, when the ballet was choreographed for me. What I learned, I teach to the young dancers. This is the way you pass ballet on from generation to generation."

I understand. There is no change, no deviation from Balanchine's directions.

"In your heart of hearts, Maria, do you ever want to dance again?"

"Ah, no. NO. I know that I can't," she cries. "You see, that constant striving for perfection was with me all of my life, and I know that I cannot do it. It's a physical impossibility. Because when I stopped dancing, I really did stop training. I still keep myself physically fit, but I do not pretend that I can do a proper *arabesque.*"

I bring up a recent magazine article that discussed among other things, the plight of the corps dancer whose basic salary is less than those of the stagehands. Some, in New York companies, have aggressively pressed for large increases in pay and benefits and won. Maria has not read the article, but union demands clearly upset her.

"We're unionized enough around here," she moans. "We don't even start to dance until two weeks from now, and we've been paying salaries, salaries, SALARIES. When I was young, we got half-salary when we rehearsed. Now they get *full* salary! And we're teaching them how to dance! That's what *kills* me.

"It is very difficult. Very difficult. It's the stupid people who don't understand. The intelligent ones know what they are getting here."

She mentions a dancer who has been with her since she was fourteen and had really blossomed. "But it takes time. *Time!* And patience on the part of the teacher and on the part of the dancer. It doesn't happen overnight.

"It's dedication. That's what it has to be with a dancer. We're not here for money. If you are here for money, then you're not going to be a dancer because it's too difficult.

"Dancing is never going to be perfect. That's impossible. Your leg hurts, your back hurts, your neck hurts, you've got an infected foot, you know? I have one girl, I've never seen anyone take care of herself the way she does. If she gets a little twinge in her knee she's out for a week. In the meantime, we have been rehearsing, *sweating* to get the work done—and her knee is hurting!

"She will fall by the wayside. And it's tragic, tragic for her, and tragic for us. Because I have spent a great deal of time on her, coaching, training, cajoling. But I cannot put *my* perseverance into her body. Tenacity. You *have* to have this. If you don't have it, you're not going to have a career.

"One thing I know about dancing. It is difficult, hard work, and that's *all*. And if God has given me talent and musicality and the right configuration, there is no reason why you cannot have a wonderful, satisfying career. Many of my friends who have never known me in those earlier times think I've had such a glamorous life. Danced for the queen and all. Yes. But I didn't realize it at the time because I was too tired! Too nervous about how I was going to dance the next day. In retrospect I can think 'Wasn't that wonderful?' but it was just back-breaking work."

Piano music begins in the next studio. She gets up to go.

One thing more before you leave. If ballet is the most ephemeral of arts, vanishing in a moment as it does, if it is a continual striving for perfection that often eludes the pursuer, if it is accompanied by hunger, exhaustion and frequent pain, where is the joy?

A great smile spreads across her face, lighting it.

"It is that ability to move in space, in time, to a certain amount of music, dancing steps that have been choreographed by the great genius of our century. It's as though you *are* the music. Even though it's not always perfect, just the fact that you can *be* there. That you have the ability to at least make the attempt to do it, that is the joy."

Did we understand?

Yes. Yes. YES.

2

THE MUSICIAN

Eugenia Zukerman

> *The Concert Flute* is a cylindrical tube but with a more or less conical head, stopped at one end. The player blows across a mouth-hole in the head and his breath, impinging on the edge of the hole, sets in vibration the column of air inside the tube. The lowest octave of the scale is produced by altering the effective length of the tube by the use of keys covering the finger holes; the next octave is produced in the same way but with increased wind-pressure, and the third octave is produced in a complicated way of "cross fingerings" that are impossible of description here. Thus there is a three-octave range.
> —*The Oxford Companion to Music*

It is a concert at a Midwestern Bible college in the waning days of winter. The audience is hungry for good sound to lift winter-weary spirits. Wearing blue jeans or black tie—as though unable to decide on the proper dress for this young, world-famous couple—they crowd the auditorium. Coiffured gray hair is everywhere, but so are pony tails and beards. A child of about three sits patiently, waiting for the music to begin.

The audience bows its head. It is probably the first time Eugenia and Pinchas Zukerman have been brought on stage with a prayer.

"Let us sing to the Lord new songs. Prophesy on new instruments . . . make a sacrifice of praise," is the fervent cry.

With that, the Zukermans appear. She walks quickly on stage, a petite blonde woman whose beauty radiates. to the back of the hall, carrying a shimmering flute aloft like a banner and radiating such a grin you are confident music *will* be made this night.

Pinchas, smiling through his beard, follows more slowly—relaxed, violin casually tucked under one arm. Samuel Sanders, their accompanist, sits down at the piano.

You were right. The Telemann Sonata in G pours into willing ears and settles into the body—the flute music hovering in the vicinity of the head, the violin in the viscera, where it makes the stomach vibrate, the fingers hum.

When they make music together, Eugenia and Pinchas seem welded. Together they play impossibly rapid passages, dazzling maneuvers where neither misses a step.

They seem to enjoy this dazzling, this reaching for and making almost impossible combinations. Though their instruments are separate, the music of each clear and "focused," as Eugenia says, it is inevitably wedded. You have the conviction that they could not play together that closely, that intimately, without being husband and wife.

Later on in the concert, Eugenia plays alone, and we are led on one of those secret, unauthorized journeys only flutes seem to be able to take. The three year old, who has been restless but polite during the violin music, is smiling as he listens to her.

At times, she seems to physically extract the music from her instrument, bending backwards, swaying left and right, leaning toward the audience to share moments of the music, standing on tiptoe, even, to reach for it.

She soars into piccolo range, explores mellow alto territory, and is at home in both, as she is in the leaps themselves. All of this is done seemingly without effort, with such a lightness that one wants to breathe for her.

The final piece is a Doppler trio for flute, violin, and piano from which the musicians emerge flushed, in high spirits.

The applause is briefly enthusiastic, there are some isolated bravos, enough for an encore, then the Zukermans and Sanders disappear.

All that music—that smorgasbord of sound is gone forever, except in the imperfect memories of those who heard it. They won't remember much more than remnants, bits of sound, an experience.

To make this music for two hours, Eugenia Zukerman left her home in New York at 1:00 P.M. for the hour ride to La Guardia, the two-hour plane ride to Chicago, another hour ride to the campus of the college, a hurried meal, to be on stage from 8:15 until 10:00. Then the flight back to New York at 11:30; home at 2:00 A.M.—so she will be there in the morning when her children wake. She does not like to leave their girls, six and eight: "I cry every time."

This concertizing life sounds exciting and fulfilling, shimmers with glamour.

Reality is flatter. For her, tonight's concert was not red hot. Months later when she looks back on it, she will not find much memorable except that the weather was very cold and she was able to do the concert in one day.

Then what makes her play forty concerts a year? As the wife of Pinchas Zukerman, one of the world's great violinists, she could preside over gracious musical evenings in her home, attended by the likes of Itzhak Perlman, Isaac Stern, Daniel Barenboim; be a loving, doting mother to the children; write a novel about the precarious life of a musician; play the flute for her own enjoyment; do her nails. The fact is, she does all of those things—except her nails—and she still plays the concerts.

It's not for the money. The money she makes is very good, but she doesn't need it. Pinchas' money is more than adequate to keep them living well all their lives.

The applause?

"It's a nice little pat on the head. Obviously you want to please this audience. Approbation is part of the impetus that makes you want to go on and do it again."

But simply said, she must do them. Cannot *not* play. It is a physical thing with her.

"If I don't play for several days, I feel tense, constricted. As if I'm suffocating."

She watches closely, as though she's wondering if you'll believe that.

But there are thousands, perhaps millions, of musicians who play for their own pleasure without giving concerts. Why concerts, that laying of self on the line, for an audience that might, as it did at the Bible college, applaud after the first movement of a sonata? "That didn't bother me," she says, and her mind suddenly is somewhere else, in a better time.

"During the year, when I play forty concerts, three of them might be, for me, sublime. Everything will be right. *That* is life affirming. It keeps me going. I can say to myself, remember Schenectady? You see, Schenectady *was* sublime. It has a wonderful old vaudeville hall that has been restored. The hall was filled with a wonderful audience. The feel of that night, the memory of it, kept me going for months." It was a recital with her husband, whom she calls Pinky, and for two hours she made music the way she enjoys it best, with him. But she will make music again, with or without him. She made music long before she met him and cannot see that she will ever stop.

"I first heard the flute when I was ten years old. A member of the Hartford Symphony had come to our grammar school to demonstrate different music instruments. The flute went right to my heart. It was the most enchanting thing I had ever heard."

She flew home to tell her parents about this magical instrument she had heard. Did they know what a flute was?

Of course they knew. Both loved music. Both played the piano; her mother had once danced professionally; her father, a nuclear physicist, had sung with David Randolph. They said simply,

"Well, let's get you one."

So it began. What kind of a little girl was this so turned on by flute music? A prodigy? Not exactly. She was the middle of three sisters, two of whom played the piano.

"I was overweight, had buck teeth (which were later straightened with braces) and a lot of energy. I remember feeling buoyant all of the time. Fairly good natured. I'm the kind of person who is either up or down—there's very little gray. But mostly I was up. Resilient. I was kind of a loner. I never really belonged to a clique of kids at school.

"From the very first moment that I played the flute, I dreamt of performing. My dream was Carnegie Hall, of course, which I had never seen. I dreamt that I would come out on the stage in a green dress and that I would play and it would be the most magical moment in my life." (In 1973, Eugenia Zukerman played a recital at Carnegie Hall. She wore a green dress.)

"Of course, that was a childish dream of the goal without realizing that the process is everything."

In a way, starting the flute at ten made the process more difficult. The flute is an extension of breathing. She was able to get a sound from the flute right away, but she did not have the breath capacity at ten, the energy that she would have later on, to refine the sound. Unlike violinists, who must begin at age five in order to develop small-muscle control, a flute player can begin later, say fifteen. Eugenia could have, but by fifteen she was already first flute in various city and state orchestras. By then she had also won all the local flute competitions there were to win.

All of them? She smiles.

"Well, I don't remember losing. Maybe one or two.

"Competitions. Everyone hates them, but it's a known fact that to get anywhere with an instrument, you have to perform competitively. Enter competitions and win them. Very few people make careers without doing this.

"I can remember challenges. I was ten years old. Eleven? You could challenge for the first flute seat in the school orchestra. I can remember the feeling in the pit of my stomach. Here comes Leslie Seldon. (I'll *never* forget her.) She wants to be first flute, and I'm not going to let her. Do you know that competitive feeling? I *am* competitive."

Wanting to play the flute, wanting to compete, was one side of the coin. Not wanting to play it was the other side. Shirley and Stanley Rich were supportive parents in the first case, adamant in the second.

"I was thirteen, and I went through a monstrous phase. I told my parents, 'I'm quitting the flute. I don't care what you say, I don't want to do this. You can't make me.'

"My father did not say the usual kind of thing. He just said, 'I'm sorry, that's out of the question. You're acting like a spoiled bourgeoise child, and I won't have it. If you refuse to study, you're going to develop into a dull, uninteresting person. You will practice tomorrow, so forget it. There is no way you're not going to play the flute.'

"I spent the day in anger and fury. It was, you see, more a character attack that he launched into rather than a 'you'll thank me later' kind of thing. I suppose I really knew what he meant because I came down for dinner feeling very tractable. I had been asking for it. That was a big lesson for me as a parent, to know that children often want you to say, 'Look, I know it's hard but you've goddam well got to do it. And that's all.'"

During her senior year in high school, Eugenia began studying with Julius Baker, principal flutist of the New York Philharmonic. There was an audition before he accepted her as a pupil.

She played part of the Prokofiev Sonata in D Major and part of the Poulenc sonata. She thought she played well. Baker asked her to play some scales. She was miffed, but she did. He listened and then told her she had a lot of work to do. She'd have to go back and learn scales and arpeggios all over again.

"Here I was, almost the number one flute player in Connecticut, and I went to New York and he says, 'Ha. You're not so hot.' That was *good* for me."

After graduation from high school, Eugenia entered Barnard College as an English major, while continuing to study once a week with Baker. But after two years, Eugenia was dissatisfied.

"I was majoring in English and there were a lot of required subjects that I didn't think would help me particularly with anything. Also, I had this sense of amateur quality of the music-making at Columbia.

"One day, after a lesson, we were sitting around. Julius Baker is more than a teacher to me. He's a dear friend. One of the wonderful things about him is he's very straightforward and says exactly what's on his mind. He said to me, 'Why do you want to fool around with fine arts? Why don't you come to Juilliard and have a *real* profession?'

"I was just ready for someone to tell me this. I needed challenge. I felt ready. I spoke to my parents about it. I visited Juilliard, saw that they had academics. I was impressed by the quality of the teaching there, and of course, I had my teacher, Julius Baker. It was like firing off another rocket. I was ready for the next stage."

Attending Juilliard was one of those life decisions that in retrospect becomes almost unbearably important. It was a decision challenged from several quarters. An English professor at Barnard told her she was ruining her life. A boyfriend insisted it was her parents who wanted her to make the change, not Eugenia.

She made the change anyway, and the difference in schools was, to her, amazing.

"At an undergraduate liberal arts school, everyone was taking this and that; there wasn't much of a feeling of urgency to do anything.

"But at Juilliard there were middle-aged people—at least they seemed so much older. And they were all *very* driven, obsessed with doing one thing very well.

"Even the academic courses I took were more stimulating in some ways than those I took at Columbia, because Juilliard students did not come with any sort of academic prejudice. They were very open, very enthusiastic."

Now, instead of required English courses, she was taking theory and harmony, ear training, the literature and the materials of music. And of course, there was continuous study with Julius Baker.

"Musicians are like sponges: I soaked up everything."

Did there come a time in your studies when you said to yourself or to your teacher, That's enough! I have to do it *my* way. Did you have to sever some kind of umbilical connection?

"No. You might say to yourself, I disagree with this, but I'm going to play it that way. Learn it his way. Then you can go out and play it your way. The battle of wills never appealed to me. I was keen to see if I could do it the way he was talking about. When I finished at Juilliard, then I felt I needed to try things on my own."

Her second year she joined the Juilliard Orchestra, not surprisingly, as first flute. Enter violinist Pinchas Zukerman, also of the Juilliard Orchestra, strings section, "way in the back," says Eugenia. Handsome, raven haired, with limpid dark eyes, Zukerman continually tried to catch the attention of the cool, blonde first flutist. She ignored him at the beginning; he persisted; a two year romance occurred; and now at her graduation, Zukerman wanted her to marry him instead of joining the Denver Symphony as first flute.

Younger than Eugenia by four years, but with a career blazing with promise as winner of the prestigious Leventritt competition for violinists the year before, Pinchas prevailed over Denver. They were married in a small synagogue in 1968, with a minimum of music. "I think we had some Bach, but I can't remember," says Eugenia. "When you're doing something as momentous as taking a vow, I didn't want music."

Soon after his triumphant debut with the New York Philharmonic, Pinchas was blanketed with invitations to play. For three glorious, extraordinary years, the Zukermans traveled all over the world as Pinchas made dazzling debuts in the capitals of Europe. Those were exciting, heady times, but fraught with emotion.

"In those early years," Eugenia admits, "I lost my own identity completely. I was so tied to Pinky that when he stood up to play, I had an anxiety attack.

"Yet I was very pleased to be with Pinky. There was nothing quite as thrilling as being with him in the major capitals of the world when he made his debut. I would never have given that up just to go play a concert myself somewhere."

But by 1970, after three years of travel, Eugenia admitted she was frustrated.

"*I* wanted to play the flute. *I* wanted to give concerts."

In short, she wanted to make her own music. She did not want to join an orchestra, for that would have meant staying in one location. That left concerts, tours, appearances—but one does not snap a finger and begin a career. No announcing, I'm ready now to solo. She could have played for various managers, hoping one would like her music-making and take over her career, but that wasn't the way and she knew it. It was back to the competitions again. On a higher level perhaps, but the same kind of challenges she knew as a child.

"Very few musicians become soloists without competitions. Pinky, for example, defied Isaac Stern, who said he didn't have to go into the Leventritt, but Pinky felt he had to. Somehow, if you make it in one of those competitions, you feel as though you've done it on your own rather than by recommendation or word of mouth. It's fierce competition. But it's a fact of a musician's life."

A long pause.

"Life itself is competitive. I've thought about the "what-ifs" in my life. I'm a person who has a lot of drive. I can imagine being unhappy, unsatisfied in a small, closed community, in a routine way of life. I don't think I have it in my nature to be a loser. There are certain personalities that are 'almosts.' You know—they are almost a person. And then there are others who try to go for gold all the time."

In 1970, Eugenia "felt ready" to go for the gold. She decided to audition for the Young Concert Artists in New York City. She would be competing against other musicians, not only flutists. There were several hundred entrants at the beginning. Her attitude about the three part competition was mixed.

Intellectually, by now she had learned that you couldn't put too much emphasis on any one part of the competition. If she got close, fine. Inside, she was secure. She felt good about herself. She was happily married, felt she would always have music in her life in one form or another. Whatever happened, she could always play. Still, over the month-long competition, nerves were fraught. A minor concern intruded on her concentration: She was wearing a miniskirt, and the stage was very high. She won the preliminaries, the semifinals, and competing against ten other musicians, the final competition. As a winner, she was given a debut concert at Town Hall in New York City, March 9, 1971, about which the *New York Times* crowed:

Few flutists have staged as enjoyable a recital as Ms. Zukerman's debut.... The secret lies in her musicianship, which is consummate, and her taste, which is immaculate. Ms. Zukerman phrases with freedom and has an uncanny knack of pointing each passage so that it creates a vacuum for the next.

She is off somewhere, reliving those good days, a broad grin staying in place. The eyes dance.

"I felt ready for that competition—but I wasn't quite sure I was *that* ready."

As a winner of the Young Artists competition, she now also had management, who began arranging concerts for her. It was at that point she began going separate ways from her husband.

"It was very hard for me. We had been together from the time we met, twenty-four hours a day. To be without him...."

Was it worth it? In those early days of playing alone, did you ever ask yourself, Why am I here, why am I doing this?

There is another of those long pauses. "Yes. It was worth it. I felt secure. Glad to be on my own. And it was terrifically exciting. While Pinky was in Paris, Munich, Vienna (eyebrows raised) there I would be in Vermillion, South Dakota. Morris, Minnesota. It was WONDERFUL." She laughs.

A little over a year later, the Zukerman's first child was born, a daughter. Eugenia had continued playing concerts and recitals, traveling until she was seven and a half months pregnant.

"I felt fine. I was just very big, but I felt natural." As she would with both children, she nursed until the babies were nine months old. This meant they went with her wherever she traveled, along with someone to look after them during rehearsals and concerts.

"Babies travel easily," she maintains and points out that nursing is a lot easier than taking along bottles. Besides, babies sleep a lot. "Certainly there were difficulties, but if you want to do something enough, you do it."

Her concerts had been small at the beginning, but over the next few years her itineraries began changing from Vermillion, South Dakota, and Morris, Minnesota, to Los Angeles, Washington, New York. The more she played, the more

people heard her and about her. Well-known conductors began asking for her, and that's the way she and Pinky had planned it.

"Early on, we decided there would be no sugar-daddy stuff. He would not say, Why doesn't my wife come along and play? We felt that was very important for our relationship."

In 1976, Eugenia renewed an acquaintance with the internationally known flutist Jean-Pierre Rampal, the man who had almost single-handedly elevated the flute to a solo instrument. The Zukermans and Rampal were playing together as part of a musical "crew" on the ship *Renaissance*. Rampal invited her to play with him and to record. The following year they recorded some Bach trios, then played together at the Chamber Music Society of Lincoln Center. Later there was a Carnegie Hall recital with him.

"Rampal is very much like Pinky in his joie de vivre. In the ease with which he makes music. He's remarkable in the way that he *encourages*. It's like playing with a really strong tennis player. You rise to the occasion and then you don't sink back."

She made a number of other collaborations—a duo with guitarist Carlos Bonnel, a trio with pianist Jerome Lowenthal and cellist Jeffrey Solow. And there were more and more appearances with Pinky. Recitals, concerts, and many solo appearances with orchestra. Does she prefer one over the other?

"I like diversity. As a soloist, when you go out and play a Mozart concerto, there's a certain loneliness. You are exposed. Alone. The focus is on you, and there is more of a burden than when you're having a dialogue with another person.

"Chamber music is the core of music making. It's like speech, and when you are out there with someone it's a team feeling.

"But I enjoy recitals because they are very demanding. The beauty of music is that the more you play it, the more you find in it—new themes you never really discovered before. And you learn, when you play concerts, that though you have moments of glory, many of them, they're not such a big deal. There is tension—and relaxation. That's what music is about. Stress that has release. It's very healthy. How else do we explain the longevity of musicians?"

When she is playing well, and she knows it, how does she feel inside?

"I don't hear myself the way you hear me. When I feel good about my sound, when I feel I'm producing the sound that is *mine*, there is a certain flowing quality I have, a suspension as if there is no flute there. It's as if I'm *really* singing. It's open and I feel golden. There's a warmth about it. Everything I want to say is being said in this flowing. It's clear. It's a focused sound. I try to spin the sound so that it goes on and on beyond the hearing, so that it doesn't just *stop*. So that it's vital."

We've been talking all this time about achievement, about doing what you feel you *must* do. Were there never any doubts, self-doubts that inhibited your ability to play?

"I had *terrific* doubts. I can remember when I first began playing, I would stand in front of an orchestra as a soloist and think, They have flute players here that can play as well as I can. With me, self-doubt is a motivating force. I'm tenacious. I would say, O.K., there *are* other flute players here who could do this, but here I am. I can do it too. I have something valid to say, something distinctive, and I know that I can do some justice to this music."

Are you making music for Eugenia Zukerman or for the audience?

"I'm really playing for myself and for the music now. In the beginning of my career I would think, Is my slip showing? Do I look alright? Do they like me? Am I playing too long, too short; am I flat, am I sharp? I was self-conscious, and the stage seemed alien territory. I felt very exposed.

"Now I am totally involved in the music. It happened about five years ago when my second child was born. My playing somehow hit another level. It was at that point my husband, for the first time in knowing him, said to me, '*That* was marvelous.' He was always encouraging; very supportive of my playing, but we both knew that there was a certain roughness there still. In any artistic process, as you grow as a person, as your life becomes more intensified—all that somehow goes into the work. It's then that you feel you've mastered it. I feel now, if you put anything on the music stand, I could learn it, perform it, and be pleased with the results.

"There's less ego gratification now. Each time I feel excitement that I'm going to be given another chance to try to say something with the instrument. That's the nice thing about concerts—endless chances."

And what about the time when things aren't good? When nothing meshes, nothing jells?

"We all start playing at small places. What do you do when the orchestra is barely recognizably playing what you're playing? There have been people who have stomped off stages and refused to play. I'm not a stomper. I've had to play, here in New York, with someone I've felt was really incompetent. There was no point in saying to him, You're not following me. I simply said to the concert master, 'Look, can I count on you to really bring the section in on time?' You learn a certain tolerance. On the other hand, you have to try not to compromise yourself."

Concertizing is an art nearly as demanding as music. What did you find going out on tour for the first time that you didn't expect?

"The debilitation that you feel from flying. The constant disorientation. You're called upon to be cordial and charming when you get off a plane and you're exhausted. That's the social pressure. And there's also the pressure of nerves, that you're going to be performing. You're on display. Above all, you have to be *ready*. Because you know your schedule so far in advance, up to a year, you have to deal with any extraneous problems *before* you get there."

If, during a concert, there is a disaster—a note cracks, perhaps, or a note is missed—are you devastated?

"As I grow older, one thing I do know. It's very painful at the moment, but I know that in a couple of hours I won't be so upset; tomorrow I will have it in a bit of perspective; and by next week I won't remember it. A note cracking—I know it's not going to ruin the performance. If you've revived yourself in a performance after totally drowning, you know you've done it before and you'll be able to do it again. You have that confidence that comes from having gone through it."

Are you ever completely satisfied with your playing?

"No. I have moments when I'm satisfied. This is true for most musicians. It's a very ephemeral thing we do. You do it, it's over, and there's nothing to hang on to, even if it's recorded. A performance is a record of the day . . . of who you are at that moment. I've had moments where I have left the stage and known I have played wonderfully. Everything has jelled and I've even totally enjoyed it."

Schenectady?

Schenectady.

Are you sad to understand that once the music is played, it has disappeared forever?

"No. It is not sad for me to play the music and have it gone immediately. Beauty doesn't last. You learn to deal with evanescence. Carpe diem." We look at each other and smile.

That is a truth we both acknowledge, have understood before. "And, of course, there is always afterglow, isn't there?" she adds. Triumphantly.

When you hear a true artist, how do you feel?

"It hits me physically. I don't think I am aware of it until after the experience, but during it you are totally taken away from time and place—transported onto another plane. You are somewhere else. You are that person's for the time of the experience. Makarova does that for me; my husband does it, too."

When you hear a young flutist who has promise, what is special, extraordinary, about what you hear?

"It happens quite often when I'm in a master class and I'm listening to a number of dutiful students and suddenly someone gets up to play. No one has told me that this is a very gifted person, but it hits you. That individual is communicating so directly. You feel it. You feel communicated to. Directly spoken to. It touches you."

Another day we talk about less lofty matters—the difficulties of practicing.

"I do like to practice now. For a long time I hated it. One time Rampal told me, 'If you're very busy and you have only fifteen minutes a day, don't just pick up something and play it. Play simple scales and arpeggios. It will be so much more valuable than playing quickly through something you know.' Before that advice I did haphazard scales and arpeggios. I had no set routine. My practicing was kind of mindless.

"Now I never pick up the flute without playing scales and arpeggios. They've become a signal on my personal channel. After I play them I feel solid. Warmed up. But if I haven't practiced, I don't feel as if my day is over."

Do you regret not having learned that simple lesson about playing scales and arpeggios years ago?

"Learning is a procedure which evolves. If someone could give you that magic formula which would make you instantly a fine artist, you would be bored. Discovery is so important in your work, in relationships. In everything you do.

"I think it was Spinoza who said that if you've come upon an idea after years of struggling with it, slowly, painstakingly, and finally come to this conclusion with great difficulty, if you then pick up a book and find your conclusion right there in front of you in a sentence, you must not think you've wasted all those years thinking this thing out for yourself. It's the process that's important.

"I get angry with music. I have often wanted to take the flute and throw it out the window. At the frustration of not getting a passage right or the frustration of not being able to play the way I feel like playing."

How do you get over this?

"I put the flute away. *Fast*."

But you must go back to the difficult passage some time. How do you work on it?

"Break it up into groupings. Play it slower. Play it in an interesting way. In different rhythms. Play it with a metronome. I began working a lot with a metronome. As a teenager I was not eager to sit and work with a metronome in a studied, metered way. But that's what I had to do when I was older. I still have to do that."

You have two small daughters. How do you manage to practice, to prepare for concerts—to say nothing of writing a novel and assorted magazine and newspaper articles?

"I've been lucky to have had help from the time they were babies. But I've always been a present momma. I can't have them in the house and not want to go to them.

"I can remember angrily practicing while one of them would be sobbing outside the door. I hate to be sexist, but it's true. Mother seems to be the one you look to when you need something. Pinky is a divine father to them but they won't go to him when he's practicing."

In 1976 she rented a fifth floor walk-up studio around the corner from her home, where she still spends about five hours a day. She practices for a couple of hours. Then she puts the flute away and sits down at the typewriter. She is currently working on her second novel. The first, *Deceptive Cadence*, was published last fall by Viking Press.

"I felt spoiled having the studio. And frightened. I was afraid I'd get into it and I wouldn't be able to play or write or do anything."

But that didn't happen. She finished her book there, after having worked on it for over two years on the road, in motel rooms, wherever she had a spare moment.

The book, not surprisingly, is about a musician who is caught between the dreams of his art and his real desire to make a personal commitment.

"It's about why we do it, what makes us get up there, about how hard it is to balance any sort of personal life with the demanding life of an artist."

How do the critics affect you?

"As a writer, I respect them. It's a remarkable thing that they do—go to a concert and tap out a report about what they've heard. But they can be damaging. I've seen them be cruel. They've been cruel to me in a number of places. But there are critics and critics. Last week I received a mezzo-mezzo review from a critic who, the previous week, had written that a pianist played *in tune!* I begin to wonder who becomes a critic. Luckily for musicians, musical criticism is just a comment on a concert. Concerts come and go and don't depend on critics.

"I still get hurt. Pinky finds it very amusing. But he is impervious to criticism, you see. He knows he does something better than anyone else in the whole world. That can give you a wonderful sense of security."

Eugenia Zukerman. You are thirty-seven years old, have two lovely, healthy daughters, a world-famous violinist husband, a career that is blooming and can go on for years, and your Carnegie Hall dream—complete with green dress—has come true. Do you still have dreams?

"I would like to be able to play from memory. I would like to get over the fear of 'black holes' in my mind. I have most of my music memorized, but I've discovered rather than go through moments of panic in which I think, 'O my god, where am I?' and distracting an audience, I will have the music there to look at when I need to."

The interviews are winding down. We have been talking in the Zukermans' New York apartment on Riverside Drive, in a living room surrounded with the accoutrements of sound—grand piano, cupboards of music, recordings, scores, stereo system.

Several times during the days, the living room doors have quietly opened, whispered summons have been hissed, and Eugenia has disappeared. Once, two lively, dancing-eyed little girls, have been admitted and introduced: Arianna and Natalia. The younger one shows us a drawing done in school. They are obviously curious about what's going on in the living room behind closed doors, but they're trying hard not to intrude. After each meeting with her daughters, Eugenia is distracted, her mind on the "Zukettes," as she calls them, another sense tuned to what's going on in the other room.

Do the girls want to play the flute?

"I want to encourage them to make music, but I want to discourage the flute. Not only because I feel there's enough competition between a mother and a daughter anyhow, but because there are too many flute players now. Other instruments might be better."

Arianna, the elder, does take piano lessons. Eugenia sits with her as she practices.

"What I do hope for my daughters is that they each have something that they *must* do. That they are burned up with motivation. Because without that, you are lost. Without something that you want to do with your life, you are nothing."

3

THE POET

Gwendolyn Brooks

"I believe poets are born, not made," I say to her.

She laughs. "You and my mother."

"And you don't?"

"I don't know your history," she answers. "But I'd say this to anybody passing in the street. 'You are a poet.' Everybody is a poet. I mean by that, all of us have deep feelings. We're happy, we're unhappy, we muse. We try to figure out things. Everything that a poet does. The only difference is that the others keep walking on down the street. Poets bother to put these things down on paper!"

"Well, there are poets, and there is Gwendolyn Brooks," I say. She smiles and does not argue.

Of all the arts, I believe poetry is the most difficult. It isn't flashy or alluring. We don't buy tickets, dress for it. Poems demand attention, concentration. Time to sit, mull, savor, think about. That extension of effort on the reader's part may often be unrewarding. Poetry is not easy to read. Even hers.

"Tell your reader *less*. Let him do a little digging," she says.

At their best, when they connect, her poems are powerful, shattering experiences. It is amazing to me that a few words, a few lines, in combustible placement, can cause gasps and longings and laughter and powerful shocks of self-recognition. I often roar when I read them: *That* I know is true. *I* have felt that. Others I read nervously, waiting for the thoughts, hitherto unthinkable, that will leap to my brain and explode. Sometimes I read her merely for the fun of her word surprises or the sound of her music.

What I do not share with her are the poems that she writes to blacks, simply because I am not black. In a way, these poems are more powerful, more painful for me than the others, because what I can understand of them is what I can never understand.

Gwendolyn Brooks has been criticized for this specialized address to blacks— mostly by whites, but also by some blacks. She points out the key word: *To*. Not *for*.

"That's a very important distinction. The word is to. My address, since 1968, has been to blacks because there is just so much I have to say to them. Now the rest of you, who are not of that persuasion, understand that you're perfectly welcome to *eavesdrop!*"

It is the old question. Is she a poet first, who happens to be black? Or is she a black, who happens to be a poet? I say, not begging the question, It does not matter. The work matters. That which explodes in me is *mine*. Much of Gwendolyn Brooks' poetry is mine.

When I think of her now, I return first to her radiant face. The remarkable eyebrows, which even in repose are raised high in expectation. She is ready for, alert to, all the signals sent in by the world. And whatever her eyes have seen— and they have seen it all—the eyebrows are still high, as if to say, whatever happens, bring it on. I'm ready.

As though to curb the expectation of the eyebrows, the mouth usually curves downward in a kind of wait and see position. That, or it is engaging in great laughs and whoops of delight. She offers no polite smiles in between. A characteristic pose of hers is one hand folded under one cheek. Watching, relentlessly.

She has two voices, one for conversation, one for delivering her poems to audiences. Though she is sixty-four, her conversation voice is that of a young girl. When she is surprised or pleased or amused, definite girlish "ohs" peal out. In a way that most adults have long since managed to suppress, Gwendolyn Brooks' voice reflects her feelings.

The reading voice is an instrument of great range that roams over her poems in surprising ways. Anyone who has read "we real cool" silently and then heard her read it is startled by the rhythms, the music, that she alone evokes.

I describe the physical Gwendolyn Brooks because unlike any of the other artists in this book, she herself *is* her art. She is poet as receiver, as translator, as creator, as deliverer. She is dependent upon no one except herself; she needs no other music than what she hears inside. Even the publishing of her poems, which had been done by others for over thirty years, is now under her jurisdiction, her control. What she experiences, what she feels, she boldly offers the world, whether or not the world gives a damn. How came this bold poet to be?

"My mother, Keziah, was my earliest, my first Encourager. She said that when I was seven years old, I brought her a page of rhymes. She was immediately impressed and said I was going to be the lady Paul Laurence Dunbar. That black poet was our household idol, so it meant a lot for her to say that.

"From the very beginning I felt that it was my destiny, to be a writer. I'd often write two, three, five poems in a day. I *enjoyed* it. I had the fun of it.

"I remember once I got angry. I was about thirteen or fourteen and tore up a story I had written. I don't know what I was mad about. But this was about the worse thing that anybody could do, according to my father.

" 'You tore up the story, Gwendolyn?' he asked in horror.

"I had that kind of support behind me all the time."

Keziah Wims Brooks had been a schoolteacher in Topeka, Kansas, before her marriage to David Anderson Brooks. They both revered education and books.

Keziah was especially strong, definite in her beliefs (she did not allow Gwendolyn to crawl as a baby), firm in her resolve that Gwendolyn and her brother Raymond be given every opportunity to stretch themselves, deepen their talents.

At eighty-seven, Keziah wrote and published her own book, *The Voice, and Other Short Stories* which stated some of the beliefs she held dear in her life: "An individual with no sense of purpose in life is unlikely to succeed." And, "Poets are born, but their success depends on aptitude, perseverance and faith."

David Anderson Brooks, the first of his family to finish high school, had one year at Fisk University, determined to be a doctor. The economic realities of black life in Chicago in the 1920s, marriage, and two children, ended David Brooks' dream. He became a janitor for a music publisher. Salary, $25 a week. During the Depression it sometimes would drop to $10 a week, and Brooks took to painting stores and apartments at night.

Keziah wrote, "Since both my husband and I had always believed welfare was only for sick and elderly people, we had never considered being on relief, regardless of conditions. Therefore, the Depression had an adverse effect on our lives."

Gwendolyn remembers frequently eating beans in those days. But she also remembers their own home on the South Side of Chicago, and Keziah keeping the holidays in beauty and tradition. There was love and structure in her life and stress on self-discipline. Above all, there was time to read and write. David was given an old desk that he brought home for his daughter.

Gwendolyn lovingly remembers it was "a desk with many compartments, with long drawers at the bottom, and a removable, glass-protected shelf at the top, for books."

She had many books. Particularly dog-eared were the "Emily" series, about a Canadian girl who wanted to be a writer as she did.

If Keziah was the encourager, school was the *dis*courager. More than once, teachers accused Gwendolyn of plagiarism.

"They felt the little compositions I wrote couldn't be *mine*. They were sure I was copying from someone." Her eyes flash, remembering.

It was Keziah who would storm down to school then, to inform the teacher in question that Gwendolyn was a better writer than even the teacher and that her daughter did not have to steal!

At home, she wrote continuously. Poems. Short stories. "All very, very bad," she says. The poems were about flowers, trees, friendships, enemyships. She was a "loner." She had friends, but felt ill at ease with the kids in school unless they were close neighbors at home. She even preferred writing to parties. And once there was a fire down the block, and everyone in the family ran to see it. Except Gwendolyn. She was busy writing.

At eleven, Gwendolyn Brooks published her first poem in the *Hyde Parker,* her neighborhood newspaper. At thirteen, her first published poem in a magazine appeared in *American Childhood.* Payment was six copies of the magazine.

She became an old hand with *Writer's Market* and began the writer's peculiar dance with the mailman--send poems out, wait for them to come back, send them out again.

She still believes this is the best way for poets to get published.

"Get a *Writer's Market* and plenty of envelopes and stamps," she trumpets to the young poets who ask her advice. "Failing that, if you still think you have a world saver, publish your own book!" She holds up one of hers. "One thousand copies cost me only $475. Then be inventive enough to think of ways to distribute them. That, of course, is where it is!"

She minimizes the disappointment of rejections, but frequently mentions the importance of inspiration. She recalls her own early encouragements.

One, at sixteen, when she gathered her nerve and sent a batch of her best poems to James Weldon Johnson. He wrote back, gratifyingly, that she had talent and feeling for poetry but she must study the work of the best modern poets, "not to imitate them, but to help cultivate the highest possible standard of self-criticism."

He also made a suggestion that she took to heart—in fact, would teach her own pupils in later years: "Do not be afraid to use the extra syllable." It sounds odd now, in an age of poetry that is not structured, bound by meter, but in those days the extra syllable was a maverick to be wondered at and used with care.

And one time, Langston Hughes came to Gwendolyn Brooks' church to read. Keziah urged a reluctant Gwendolyn on him afterwards, clutching a batch of her poems. He kindly read them on the spot and said that she was talented and *must* go on writing. Who could know that years later, Langston Hughes would dedicate a book of his poetry to her.

She had two years at Woodrow Wilson Junior College (now Kennedy-King) and then it was out into the real world in her first job—typist for a "spiritual advisor," who was located in the Mecca. The Mecca was a huge apartment complex at 33rd and State on Chicago's South Side. No one ever knew how many people actually lived there. Some said one thousand, some said two thousand. Gwendolyn's job, along with four other typists, was not only to type. She was to answer letters sent in by worried clients about what to do with their lives, their boyfriends.

"We were like Ann Landers," she roars.

The five typists also typed whole pages of numbers. When a client sent in a dollar, his "lucky" number was clipped from the page, put into an envelope, and sent back to him. The typists filled little boxes with bright colored powders and bottles with liquids—potions that they delivered to the clients in the building. "Paycheck Elixir, Drawing and Holding Power, Policy Number Compeller."

She hated the job, despised the lies. But she needed the money—$8 a week, of which $2 went to her parents. And though she was scarcely aware of it, the Mecca was soaking into her open pores, settling into her poet's soul to be delivered years later as her great, savage epic of black life in the ghetto, *In the Mecca.*

Eight months after she had begun, she was fired from her job because she had finally refused a bigger lie—to act as the spiritual advisor's "assistant pastor."

"I needed the money. But I was so GLAD to be released from that awful situation. And I did think, someday, I'd have to write about what I saw in the Mecca."

She began it as a novel, but found she was on "wobbly ground" with fiction and put it away. After eight years, she began once again and, in 1968, at last delivered herself of those painful months in the Mecca.

In 1939, Gwendolyn married Henry Blakely, a man who understood and shared her passion for poetry. Money was scarce, would always be in those early years of their marriage; poems were not. Gwendolyn wrote wherever they lived, in one room apartments, in kitchenettes where they shared a bathroom with the other tenants, in dark apartments where the mice poured out of the radiators in droves, but where she could look out her windows and find material for poetry. She did put her pen down for a year, she remembers, when her first child, Henry, Jr., arrived.

Then it was 1941, a quiet beginning of sorts.

Inez Cunningham Stark, a wealthy, socially prominent white woman who loved poetry, announced she would hold a Poetry Workshop for Negro "would-be" poets to be conducted at the South Side Community Art Center.

Her white friends were horrified. She would be raped going into black neighborhoods! Killed in all probability. Besides, she would never be able to teach "them" poetry. "They"—Negroes—didn't have poetry in them. Rhymes, maybe, but not poetry.

Fifteen "Negro" poets joined her class, including Gwendolyn and Henry. It was during those classes that Gwendolyn grew to love skeletons and no fat in poetry. The class often brutally criticized each other's work. Comments from Inez would come back on the poems:

"All you need ... are the last four lines!"
"You must be careful not to list the obvious things ... use them only to illustrate boredom and inanity."
"I don't understand too well what it's all about but it has three FINE lines."

Gwendolyn was exhilarated by the criticism. Undaunted.
"Young people these days say they get discouraged. That's a foreign language to me. I *never* was discouraged. And that was because I enjoyed what I was doing. Even if I had known that I was never going to get anywhere, poetry was something I loved doing. Expressing myself. I didn't get discouraged the way these young fatalists do."

She soon joined a poetry-writing class at Northwestern University, where Paul Angle "made me doubly aware of the outworn usages that were running WILD in my poems." She is laughing as she remembers, but she points out, she learned to shun the cliche, excise it from her poetry.

Are poetry workshops, poetry classes good for poets? It sounds as though you think they are.

"They are good for people who know next to nothing about writing poems. You will be taught not to use cliches, you will be taught to compose a sonnet—

you know, ABABCDCD. You can get experience in writing ballads, and you come out of a writing class that is *allowing*—because there are many writing classes that are not *allowing*—you come out of such a class with *excitement*. And then you're ready to try some things on your own. Classes and workshops are not the last answer. Just something along the way that might help a bit."

Was it difficult for you to show new work to people?

"NO. NO! I was glad to show it. That's why I was writing it! I wanted it to go out into the world. I still feel the same way."

What if a reader doesn't understand what you've written or gets something from it other than what you intend? How do you feel about that?

She lets out a whoop of delight.

"I would like for people to *get* what I'm driving at, but after you've been doing this for so long, you're happy when a person reads your poem and says that means so much to them. For *whatever* reason! Whatever they get out of it is theirs!

Tell how your first book of poems came to be published, we ask.

It was 1943. She had won the prize for poetry in the Midwestern Writer's Conference and was approached by an editor from Knopf. Did she have enough poems for a book?

Did she? After writing for almost twenty years? She sent off forty of her best. Although they were rejected, the editor liked the "Negro" poems.

Too shy to try that door again, she gathered nineteen of those "Negro" poems and sent them off to Harpers. Editor Elizabeth Lawrence became enthusiastic, wrote back, and "told me I'd have to write *more*, because nineteen poems were too small for a book. Elizabeth also said 'Take your time, you don't need to rush. Take a year, take two years.'

"But I RUSHED. I was afraid in two years they'd forget about me. In one year!"

Gwendolyn went into retirement. At that time, the Blakelys were living in a tiny kitchenette apartment above a real estate agency at 623 East 63rd St. The one with the mice and the common bathroom. No more parties; no more movies, her favorite entertainment. She wrote and wrote and wrote.

In less than three months, there were eleven new sonnets and the brilliant "Sundays of Satin Legs Smith" to add to the original nineteen. Included in this group were "The Mother," Brooks at her most clear eyed; several ballads of childhood; a poem about a lonely God, which was subsequently banned in Nebraska and West Virginia; a powerful poem on the cooling down of a marriage; an elegy for a plain black boy on his way to the cemetery. These are startling portraits of people etched in words, alive on the page in their loves and pain, strengths and weaknesses.

When the poems were accepted for publication by Harper and Brothers, Gwendolyn rushed to the common bathroom and locked herself in, to be alone with the joy, the "gold" of acceptance.

The author's copies of her book soon followed.

"I can really recall that moment, after wanting it for so long. You know, that's all I wanted to do in my life. Publish a book of poems. Just *one* book is all I wanted."

She looks at me for a long time, then shakes her head as though she still doesn't believe it.

When you look back at your work, does it age well for you?

"Indeed! I'm constantly amazed at that. And certain poems that I would have considered to be dated by now keep coming back. A poem like 'The Mother.' That subject [abortion] is in the headlines every day."

When she reads this poem in public she will sometimes preface it by saying that no, *she* has never had an abortion, and "it is a poem that is neither for or against. It is not intended to take a stand on the issue.

"Interestingly enough, both sides have asked me to let them use the poem as a standard bearer. But I won't let it be used in that way ... Yet how should I feel about this?" she asks.

"One young woman told me the poem had meant a great deal to her at a certain time in life when she was trying to decide what to do. So she decided to have the baby, and she said the result of that decision was there with her that night. Would I like to see him? And she brought me this little baby that she said was here on account of *me*! A beautiful little baby. And I HELD him!"

She makes a cradling motion of her arms and seems delighted that her poem had meant new life.

"But," she adds, "when I sit down to write, I don't have in mind 'saving the world.' Or saving anybody! I'm glad if that should happen. But I get an idea, an impression, or I'll see something that stirs me very much, and I try to put down on paper how I responded."

Her first book of poetry, A *Street in Bronzeville*, brought Gwendolyn Brooks national attention: "Gifted, passionate and authentic." "A good book, a real poet." "To use one of her own phrases, Miss Brooks 'scrapes life with a fine-tooth comb.'" Her poetry "strikes one with the force and power of her compatriot, Richard Wright's prose." Thus went the reviews.

Another book of her poems came in 1949. *Annie Allen*. In this one, Gwendolyn Brooks seemed to concentrate on technique more than substance. She wanted to dazzle. In an interview for *Contemporary Literature* she said, "I wanted every phrase to be beautiful. I was very conscious of every word. Every one was worked on and revised, tenderly cared for. More so than anything else I'd written and it is not a wild success. Some of it just doesn't come off. But it was enjoyable."

Before publication, Elizabeth Lawrence gave the *Annie Allen* poems to another poet to read, whose name Gwendolyn was not supposed to know.

"I think Elizabeth was somewhat uneasy; she felt that some of the poems were a little pretentious, didn't see them sitting well with the easy-going, poetry-reading public."

The anonymous reader/poet (who shall remain anonymous) was cool to the *Annie Allen* poems, thought some of them "tortuous," not subtle enough; suggested others be left out.

Gwendolyn put her foot down. "*No.* I want those poems left in because they make sense of certain other inclusions—there's more of a coherence there," she told her editor.

"Elizabeth was ready to accept anything I insisted on, so that's the way the book was published."

When *Annie Allen* won the Pulitzer Prize for Poetry in 1950, Gwendolyn had the last laugh.

"I'm afraid I was a little nasty at that point. *'You see?'* I pointed out. *'I was right!'* Harper never submitted any of my poems afterward for somebody to read—or if they did, I was never told."

Did Harper ever change a word in any of her poems?

"OH NO!" she cries, horrified that such a thing is even thought of. "*Never!*"

Then, "Did I tell you how I heard about the Pulitzer?" she asks, eyes dancing.

"We were living out at 9134 Wentworth, and the lights were out because our electric bill hadn't been paid. Jack Star, then a reporter on the *Chicago Sun Times*, called and said, 'Do you know you have won the Pulitzer Prize?'

"I don't believe it. I DON'T BELIEVE IT." She and son Henry, Jr. danced wildly around the house, and then they all went out to a movie to celebrate. Looking back, it seems like a minor way to celebrate a prize given to the first black in the Pulitzer history. Gwendolyn shrugs.

"It is wonderful to have awards. Almost nobody's going to reject them. But you don't live for awards. You do your work as best as you can and *enjoy* it. That's what is most important. Then, if awards come, you take 'em. A lot of people have ruined their lives because they have felt nothing was important *but* the awards. That's too bad."

In 1951, daughter Nora was born. There had been eleven years between the two children. The poems did not stop.

"When Henry was a baby, I wrote when he was asleep, and when he was older, I would write when he was in school.

"When Nora came, she was such a lovely baby. She gave me no trouble whatsoever. She would take her nice little naps. And I would write. We'd go out to the park, sometimes, and I at least would be able to make notes, think of phrases that I might be able to use.

"No, I didn't have any problems finding time to write with the children." She laughs. "Lawyers will. People who have to go out to work will. If you're writing *War and Peace*, you might have a problem. But if you're home writing a poem or two, now and then?"

"Of course, some of the great critics might say, Well, that's why you haven't become a better writer than you are. That might be true. I don't know." She grins.

As her children grew up, Gwendolyn Brooks was growing, too. She was seeing blacks in a white world from a different point of view.

Up through the early 1960s, Gwendolyn Brooks says that her poetry was in her "integration-favoring stage. Which said that if blacks were nice enough, quiet enough, took lots of baths, we would be treasured here in America." In those days, in those poems, she says she was "pleading with Americans to admit me to our mutual estate—to love us [blacks] other than curios."

The Bean Eaters, published in 1960, was clearly impatient with the slowness, the ineffectiveness of integration. There were angry poems, despairing poems, poems that spoke of the futility and frustration of black lives. "Bronzeville Woman in a Red Hat" superbly examines the earth-shaking idea of a black woman kissing a white child on the lips! (The world survived.)

The Emmett Till murder aroused an anger in the poet that would not let her rest until she wrote "A Bronzeville Mother Loiters in Mississippi. Meanwhile, a Mississippi Mother Burns Bacon."

"I had to write about it. I couldn't get any rest until I put down on paper what I thought, what I felt.

"That boy, Emmett Till, was fourteen years old, and my own son was fourteen at the same time. They said that this boy was walking down a country road and saw a pretty young woman standing in a doorway and flirted with her. Said something IMpudent. (Her voice rises dangerously.)

"I don't know what it was he said. I knew that I had a son who was impudent like all kinds of other boys at fourteen. The same thing could have happened to him.

"If I had been writing that poem now, it would have been written differently. I wrote it from the standpoint of this young white woman. I made her very human. I made her shrink from having her husband touch her after the trial was held because his hands had been in that boy's blood and he was so *proud* of what he had done."

Several people, including Southerners, told her after reading the poem that she had been wrong to make the white woman's response humane.

"Today, if I were writing it, I would write it from the boy's viewpoint, perhaps, or the mother of the boy. Her life got worse and worse after that, I heard," she says softly.

The Bean Eaters met with complete silence for months. When they finally did review the book, the reviewers thought it "too social!" From the hindsight of the 1980s, it is difficult to understand the stony silence of this book's reception. Much stronger, much angrier poems would follow, but *The Bean Eaters* had strayed off the path where readers, mostly white, had placed Gwendolyn Brooks, Negro.

We must mention here a short poem that was included in *The Bean Eaters* and has since become a classic. It is included in many anthologies as the true, representative Gwendolyn Brooks. Only twenty-four words long, it brilliantly paints the tragic past, present, and future of a gang of seven pool players. Once, at a party, Gwendolyn heard someone say "we real cool." It stuck in her mind. Years later, walking by the northeast corner of 75th and Cottage Grove, she saw a pool hall and thought, How do seven pool players feel about themselves? The result was "we real cool."

She likes the poem but wishes the anthologists "would choose something else from all that I've done. Still, that's the kind of poem you don't write any more of," she says wistfully.

In the 1960s she began to teach. There were courses at Columbia College, Northeastern Illinois State College, the University of Wisconsin, City College of New York.

"I taught a lot of creative writing and tried very hard not to get my students to write like I do. I would *announce* that. If anybody saw me heading in that direction, I told them, WATCH FOR IT AND DON'T ACCEPT IT!"

But what really can a teacher teach a poet?

"I had them read Elizabeth A. Drew's *Poetry: A Modern Guide to Its Understanding and Enjoyment*, Edmund Wilson's *Axel's Castle*, Stephen Henderson's *Understanding the New Black Poetry*.

"Books can give you an idea of what you shouldn't be doing.

"As I said, a teacher can tell you cliches are dispensible. You can be taught that."

But she said it best in an interview with Paul Angle, her former poetry class teacher.

"A teacher cannot create a poet. But ... a teacher can oblige the writing student to WRITE!"

And. "A writer needs to read almost more than his eyes can bear, to know what is going on, and what *has* gone on; not only in his own field but in related fields. And a writer needs general knowledge. And a writer needs to WRITE. And a writer needs to live richly with eyes open, and heart, too."

The interview with Angle took place in the summer of 1967. That spring, Gwendolyn Brooks had attended a Black Writer's Conference at Fisk University. The conference amazed her; it would change her life and the direction of her poetry.

"At Fisk, I met a lot of young black people who were feeling their—can I call it—black oats? Remember, this was in 1967, and all kinds of things were happening. I liked this new independence and spunk that they had. They weren't craven, you know, or slump shouldered. They had as a motto, black poetry is poetry written by blacks about blacks to blacks. That INSPIRED me, this new pride in self."

The following year she brought out *In the Mecca*, the material of which had smouldered inside her for years. Some "black" poems in the book spoke to gang members; another wondered how a black ghetto boy could possibly gaze upon the Statue of Liberty; another exhorted blacks to "conduct their blooming in the noise and whip of the whirlwind."

The poems were criticized by many whites and some blacks as being too "polemical." There will always be purists who insist that a poem need only *be* for its own sake, that the poet's role is not to instruct.

Gwendolyn Brooks does not agree with that.

"I want to speak more and more effectively to black people. All kinds of black people. My address, since 1968, has been *to* blacks because there is just so much I have to say to them. Isaac Bashevis Singer is a Jew. He writes about Jews, to Jews. No one scolds him for that. No one objects to that."

The technique conscious poet of *Annie Allen* was now saying, "Real poetry comes out of the mouths of the street." And, "In my poems I want to include music, imagery, picture, philosophy, lyricism, humor. But I want to offer them to people who may not have been able to go to college."

She did, in fact, organize a writing workshop among members of the Blackstone Rangers, a once-powerful Chicago street gang. She, and a number of young black poets whose interest was also addressing blacks, went into the South

Side of Chicago with their messages.

"We would go around to the parks, to the taverns, to Cook County jail even, and read our poems. 'We're going to lay some poems on you,' we'd say as we came in. In such a situation, what do you offer? You *don't* offer love poems such as Sara Teasdale wrote, Edna St. Vincent Millay wrote. You have to speak to them in terms that seem relevant to what they know of life. You have to have a poem that they can take to immediately. That will make them stop their drinking temporarily to listen to!"

Lean and potent, her new poems spoke directly to blacks in a new voice. She also decided to leave Harper in favor of a black publisher, Broadside Press, headed by her friend, poet Dudley Randall.

"He was giving a platform to a lot of young black poets, people who were not being accepted by Doubleday, Random House, Harper. I was urging young writers to favor this black press. Send your work to them, help them out. Finally, it got so that they had so many submissions, they couldn't publish everything they got. But at the time, they needed the faith of young blacks. So it didn't seem right for me to stay nicely, neatly in the Harper harbor while I was urging others to go to Broadside. It was something I *had* to do. Harper understood that, has always understood that." She stresses their still amiable relationship.

"Harper always made it possible for me to be as open as I wanted to be. They never censored anything. They never said you better not write this because the public might react this way or that. But, still in all, when you're dealing with a big, commercial publisher, you censor yourself."

At Broadside there would be no self-censorship. In her autobiography, *Report From Part One*, Gwendolyn Brooks was free to write firmly:

There is indeed a new black today. He is different from any the world has known. He's a tall-walker. Almost firm. By many of his own brothers he is not understood. And he is understood by no white. Not the wise white; not the schooled white, not the kind white. Your least pre-requisite toward an understanding of the new black is an exceptional Doctorate which can be conferred only upon those with the proper properties of bitter birth and intrinsic sorrow. I know this is infuriating, especially to those professional Negro-understanders, some of them *very* kind, with special portfolio, special savvy. But I cannot say anything other, because nothing other is the truth.

With her "new consciousness," she was finding that being a poet was often not enough. She wanted to do something, especially for young people. The opportunity came in 1969 when she was named poet laureate for the state of Illinois, succeeding Carl Sandburg.

"I felt a "poet laureate" should do more than wear a crown. I've made of that honor something useful."

Each year, for the past thirteen years, Gwendolyn Brooks has sponsored the poet laureate contests. She awards $500 (her own money) to outstanding young poets of elementary and high school age in Illinois.

While we've been talking in the humidity of a July heatwave, Gwendolyn Brooks has left her living room from time to time to find certain books and articles pertinent to our conversations. This time she leaves and returns with a packet of poems, her latest poet laureate winners.

"You are going to find these so *interesting*," she booms, waving them.

"How do you feel when you read the promising poetry of your young laureates?" I ask.

"DELIGHTED. I want to congratulate them for having been able to *manage*. You are always glad to know that when you're gone, poetry is going to be carried on."

Do young poets ask her advice? Do they! She points to a pile of mail on its way to the post office. She answers every letter she receives from poets, young and otherwise, seeking advice.

"What do I tell them?" She sings out in melodious tones:

"Read, read, read. Write, write, write. Live, live, Live! Of course when I say that, I should perhaps add qualifiers. *Cleanly* live!

"Don't be afraid to think for yourself. *BE* yourself. Speak most personally of *your* own illusions. Make your reader believe that what you say *could* be true."

"Should a poet listen to the advice of others or only to his own inner advice?"

"Suppose that inner advice tells you, as so many students have told me, that the way they write a poem is the way they want it to stay. After it has come out, they think, nothing more can be done. They don't want to revise. I think that is *always wrong*.

"You might write a poem that might stay the way you first wrote it, but that's rare. It is certainly rare with me. I think you ought to ask yourself, 'Can anything be done to change this? To make it closer to my original compulsion?'

"It is *never* easy writing poetry. The interest is in getting down on paper what you *really* feel. That's very difficult to do. To be honest and to see to it that your vision is honest. A thousand things might try to influence you otherwise, but that's your duty. That's your obligation. To see honestly and to report honestly what you have seen honestly. You keep at it until you say HEY! *That* approx–i–mates"—and she draws the word out to its musical width—"what I had inside.

"I don't have a single favorite poem of mine. I like stanzas here, lines there, phrases there, but one of those that I feel I have done everything I should have done with it is "The Life of Lincoln West.""

"And when the writing is going well and you feel you are catching that approximation, how are you feeling inside?"

"EXHILARATED. Those *few* times that you feel it is going well."

"That is not often?"

"Oh no. *NO.*" She stares at me in wonder.

"Then what is the joy of being a poet?" I must ask it.

"The exhilarating *agony* of putting down—taking out of yourself and putting

it down on paper. Exhilarating agony is what it really is, continues to be, and always *will* be!"

It is getting hotter. I am perspiring freely as we talk about the work of the poet. She looks as cool and refreshed as when we began.

"In bad times, in times of trouble," I begin—and she interrupts urgently.

"We're in them. Right now!"

"Yes, we are," I agree. "In the midst of these times, do you ever think to yourself, Why do I bother? What good is a poem in this kind of a world?"

"Oh *no*. I *never* think that! Often poems have really influenced trends, influenced bad times and good times. And not just poems. I was thinking today of the essay "Common Sense," which had a *great* effect upon people."

Still, I think of a poem she wrote in 1975, "A Boy Died in My Alley," in which the poet accepts the universal responsibility for the death of a stranger. It is a powerful poem, based on a true happening, but writing it clearly was not enough for her. For four years after that murder, Gwendolyn Brooks held a Saturday morning forum for teenagers on her block.

"What I wanted for them was a forum where they could say *anything* that popped into their heads. Tell anything before the group that disturbed them, that they wanted out in the open. The reason I started this club was because when the police came and asked us if we had known the identity of this boy found dead in our alley, we had not. It was quite a shock. I asked the kids if they had known this boy, and the report was that some of them had known him, a little bit. He was morose, always in trouble, and kept to himself.

"I don't know what caused his death, but it made me think that somebody should be in touch with the rest of these kids, get them together, get them to liking each other. Because in those days, they were just passing each other, maybe saying hi and maybe not."

The Saturday morning forum lasted four years, until the kids graduated from high school. As each graduated, Gwendolyn gave a cash scholarship or a trip to Africa. Two went to Africa. The rest accepted scholarships.

"I give a lot of awards and scholarships." She laughs. "My husband thinks I'm crazy to be giving awards."

"Is poetry that lucrative?"

No, but lecturing is. Nowadays, Gwendolyn Brooks spends a lot of time lecturing at universities all over the country. There are usually fifty or so such visits a year where she chairs a seminar in poetry, conducts poetry workshops or lectures, and reads her poetry. But she cannot—has never been able to—support herself writing poetry.

"I never tell anyone that. It's *impossible*. I have so many books out now that the royalties that I make, though very modest, would feed me. Yes. I could be fed. But I couldn't begin to do the kinds of things that I like to do for young people. The lectures allow me to do that."

I tell her that what knocks me out about her is that she is so *sure*.

"Of what?"

Of yourself. Of what you do.

"Oh. Well." She answers in a high, delighted voice. "I'm sixty-four years old. When Eve [our ten-year-old daughter who has come with us on one of the interviews] is sixty-four, *she'll* be sure, too!"

"You never have doubts that what you say is important? Never did?"

"No. I feel that what I'm saying is important AND valid, and although if we had certain critics in the room whom I've met, they would shriek and shudder to hear me say 'useful,' I believe that much that I have written has been *useful*. I'm afraid that I join Emily Dickinson in saying, 'If I can keep one heart from breaking. . . . ' " She laughs.

"Do those critics matter to you?"

"Absolutely not. They used to. I used to *watch* for reviews. Wanted to write poetry that would bowl them over. No longer. I have written something that is a lifeline for myself. A credo. If you believe it—and I hope you do—that credo will tell you that I must do what I feel ought to be done. Whatever the critics say! That credo is, 'Conduct your blooming in the noise and whip of the whirlwind.'

"You know, when I got to be sixty, I said to myself, *now* I am not going to do anything I don't want to do, unless I see a very good reason for it. When you get older, it's time to cut out the things that really make you miserable or that you don't like doing for one reason or another. I really hate parties with mobs of people standing around with a cocktail in hand, saying NOTHING.

"I love being with myself. And as I grow older, I love that more than anything else. There are so many things to think about and work out. To really *look* at things, including my own interior. So I often sit and *think!*" She beams at me.

"You are a happy woman, aren't you?"

"I don't really care for the word 'happy.' I often feel as though I could use the word, but I don't think we ought to aim for continuous states of happiness. I am a firm believer in loving life. I like the word 'enjoy' much better. There is certainly a lot in this world to enjoy as well as to agonize over."

The eyebrows are high, and this time the mouth is smiling.

Her telephone, which is set to buzz softly, buzzes and buzzes. I point out that someone is calling, thinking she has not heard it.

"Oh, I'm sure they'll call again." She laughs at my look of wonder at not answering the telephone, a skill I'll never master.

The last time I saw Gwendolyn Brooks was at a poetry reading and lecture at Roosevelt University. It was a day to honor her, a special Gwendolyn Brooks day, and slightly ironic because in the sixties, Roosevelt University had refused to allow Gwendolyn Brooks to teach there because she had no degree. Before she began the reading, Gwendolyn Brooks said a few words about herself and her background, believing there might be some in the audience who did not know who she was.

She told us modestly, "I think of myself as ordinary. But beautiful."

The applause was deafening.

THE OPERA SINGER

Roberta Peters

It has always seemed a miracle to me, whose singing voice is devoid of any pitch or tone, that most human beings can sing and do.

An even greater miracle is how we sing. It is one of those exquisite mysteries of nature, like seeing, that man really does not understand at all. We know that the brain silently imagines a sound, then directs two tiny vocal cords, each less than a half inch long, to produce the imagined sound by tightening or slackening in minute degrees. The lungs, of course, supply the air that sets the tiny cords vibrating, and the chest and neck and mouth resonate the sound, but singing is basically a secret contract between the brain and vocal cords. Add the emotional impact of the singer's heart and mind and a composer's intent, and the effects are stupendous!

Those two little cords, vibrating at the will of an artist, can convey human beings to heights and depths of emotion as no other sound can; a human voice singing at the very limits of its power can bind us in an intense union with strangers in an audience, even though not one of us understands the words being sung.

No one is more in awe of those "two little strings" than Roberta Peters; no one can give more fervent witness to their power than she who has been using them to touch her fellow human beings for thirty years.

One of those human beings she touched recently was a critic who wrote:

At first, Miss Peters' voice seemed a little light, then it began to soar out above the accompaniment and the final two songs (Richard Strauss) became magnificent collaborations between soloist and orchestra ... what she gave her listeners went far beyond appearance. It was a sense of enjoyment of music, a warm generosity of spirit that seemed more truly Viennese than the program. There was death, poverty and the threat of war in the Vienna of long ago but their answer was dazzling music and an affirmation of life. Miss Peters brought this indomitable vitality to glorious life Thursday night, like a beacon in our own mean-spirited time.

This, then, is the story of the keeper of one set of remarkable cords and what she has done with them. . . .

They won't ever make a movie of her life. It's too corny. But if they do, it will go like this.

Opening scene, a dining room in Grossinger's, the popular Catskills resort. Time: the early 1940s. Metropolitan Opera star Jan Peerce (frequenter of Grossinger's) is being buttonholed by maitre d' Leon Hirsch. Will Peerce please listen to Hirsch's twelve-year-old granddaughter sing and deliver an opinion on her voice to the family?

With heaven-help-me glances (does everybody in the world have a granddaughter?), Peerce consents to listen. To his surprise, little Roberta Peterman *is* good. She has a sweet, pure voice in the coloratura range. Don't let her be a prodigy, he warns. No singing of heavy stuff. Get with a good teacher. If she does these things, he tells the family, there's a possibility of an operatic career. Exit Peerce.

So Roberta studies diligently for seven years (calendar pages flip by) and grows up into a beautiful nineteen-year-old. Reenter Peerce. He listens to her sing again. Now he's *really* excited by the pure and trained coloratura voice he hears. He's so excited he arranges for impresario Sol Hurok to hear her. And Hurok is so impressed that he arranges an audition with Rudolph Bing, general manager of the Metropolitan Opera.

You guessed it. An enthralled Bing quickly grants the nineteen-year-old Roberta Peterman (now Peters) a contract with the Met. That's not all.

Now it is a morning three months before Roberta's scheduled debut. The star of *Don Giovanni* phones in with the news that she has food poisoning (what else?) and won't be able to sing that night. Bing calls Roberta in. A little emergency. Can she help them out? Can she sing the Zerlina role? Of *course* she can! With just five hours notice, Roberta Peters, who has never sung one note in public, much less one on the Metropolitan stage, grabs a subway (rush hour, she can't get a cab), goes on in the star's place, and makes her debut.

The petite, unknown coloratura from the Bronx is an instant smash. Photographers crowd into her dressing room afterwards; flashbulbs pop as Roberta, her beaming parents, her teacher, and Rudolph Bing direct wide, finale smiles into the camera. A new star is born! The end. And the beginning. . . .

You see? That's too corny. We demand our movies today have real life endings. We know there is certainly not happiness. We expect broken marriages, drifting children, excesses of body, and privations of spirit. The familiar too much, too soon syndrome.

So it is with a bit of reluctance that we travel to Scarsdale, New York, to meet her, to find our what really happened after the closing credits. Thirty years have passed.

We know that she has had the same husband for twenty-six years, Bertram Fields. They have two handsome, grown sons. She frequently sings to raise money for Bonds for Israel and the Cystic Fibrosis Foundation; she gives forty concerts a year, knocks Middle America dead with her "Merry Widow." She has sung at the White House for six different presidents, and she's thrilled every time. She has remained with the Metropolitan Opera thirty years. Thirty years, mind you; five hundred performances in those famous halls. Knowing all this, we are sure she will be a brunette Doris Day. Too good to be true.

Her home doesn't help. It is sumptuous Tudor. Twelve rooms. Elegant, carefully chosen antiques. Grand piano, swimming pool. Gardens. A tennis court. And Roberta Peters herself, dazzling in a pink and lavender outfit that picks up the deep blue of her eyes. She is fifty-one and she looks ten years younger. This body, in this setting, does not suggest difficulties. Hard work. Discipline. Decisions.

Ah, Roberta of the laughing blue eyes and low chuckle. You are not all surface, thank God. Under that trim, matched, and coordinated exterior is a cool, refreshing realist. Dispeller of myths.

"I never dreamed, as a kid, that I would be singing at the Met. I didn't know anything about opera in those days. Who knew from what? I knew *movies*! I thought I might like to be a movie star!"

She and her parents and grandmother lived in a fourth floor walk-up in the Bronx. They were not "poor," but both parents worked, Solomon Peterman as a shoe salesman in the Bronx, Ruth as a milliner. Roberta, their only child, a bit spoiled, protected, stayed safely home with her grandmother. And Sundays they all went to the movies together.

"Sure, I sang. *Soap* commercials!—Along with the radio." But you had to begin somewhere, we press. Where did you learn the arias that you first sang for Peerce and later for William Herman when he accepted you as a pupil? Children don't learn "Ah, fors' è lui" from *Traviata* and "Vissi d'arte" from *Tosca* all by themselves.

What we want, we tell her, are the bare bones of the Cinderella story, not just the scenario that everyone has heard and cheered. We want to know about decisions made early on, and the work involved, and how teacher William Herman influenced her. Because if Peerce was the catalyst in the making of Roberta Peters' voice, William Herman was surely the moving force behind it. Peerce had heard of William Herman through Patrice Munsel, a young singer who had recently made her debut with the Metropolitan, and had suggested the Petermans call him.

At the mention of Herman, there is hesitation. She shakes her head, remembering.

"Herman had been a singer himself, not very successful. He had put all of his training, all of his knowledge into Patrice Munsel, who was his first big star. In a way, she disappointed him. They would work very hard on her lesson, and as soon as she walked out of the studio, she would sing pop stuff. She was a very natural girl, and that's what she enjoyed singing. Herman was hurt by that, upset.

"When I came along, I became his whole life. It was a most unusual relationship. He was fifty. I was thirteen. We were together practically six days a week, for seven years. He would come up to the Bronx. My grandmother would

cook for him. He was father figure, teacher figure, authority figure. I loved him tremendously. I looked up to him. I respected him."

At that first meeting, however, it is doubtful that either Herman or the Petermans knew it would be an audition to change all their lives.

Roberta was nervous. She sang the same heavy material she had sung for Peerce, arias from *Tosca*, *La Traviata*. Long afterward, Herman remembered thinking at the time it would be "years before she would get a chance at 'Ah, fors'è lui' again."

"Then he took me up to those very, very high notes. I would vocalize with him A above high C," which, she explains, is not that hard for a young voice. "I had those extreme high notes, which impressed him, but I had not much middle voice."

She also sang for him a simple Scottish folk song, "Bonnie Sweet Bessie," ending on an exquisite pianissimo A flat. It was that song, that note, that convinced Herman that behind the voice was a true feeling for music.

In range, she was a coloratura, the highest of all sopranos. A trained coloratura voice is flexible, light, and capable of singing dazzling virtuoso passages, trills, runs. Herman was excited by it and its possibilities. He also knew it could be easily ruined. He was of the old school. Make haste slowly. They would take it *very* slow. For the present she would not sing anything. Then they would begin with notes. No songs. Just notes. In scales. In two note trills. She learned how to sustain a note; then crescendos and decrescendos, and mastery of the long phrase.

She learned the grace notes a coloratura uses—*acciaccatura*, *mordenti*, *gruppetti*. She loved the words and learning how to do what they meant.

Herman took Roberta to her first operas. *The Marriage of Figaro* (with Ezio Pinza, she remembers), *Lucia di Lammermoor*. She was entranced. *Lucia* became her favorite opera and later would be the first role she learned.

What Herman taught, Roberta "soaked up like a sponge and came back the next time ready for more. If I didn't have a lesson, I would go up to Herman's library and sit for hours listening to his Galli-Curci records, Tetrazzini, all the great coloraturas. Ah, Galli-Curci, isn't she a beauty? Small. Tiny. She caresses every sound."

Several months after Roberta began lessons with Herman, there was a major crisis in her life. As a graduate of Wade Junior High School in the Bronx, she was now eligible to take the citywide examination for the High School of Music and Art. The exam consisted of both a singing and a written part. She, her family, her school teachers, and her friends were certain she would be accepted. She was not. To this day, she doesn't know why.

"All I know is I failed. And it was a turning point in my life."

She fled to Herman, devastated. "And do you know what he said?" she asks, still incredulous after all this time. "He told me that Giuseppi Verdi had been turned down when he applied for admission to music school, above all not to worry, and that he had a plan."

Herman called her parents in. He announced that he was willing to take over Roberta's entire education. In addition to singing, she should study French, Italian, German, and he had the teachers lined up. He told the Petermans he would give Roberta a partial scholarship, but he wanted them to "feel a part of my career, part of my life." They agreed to pay $80 a month for her lessons. It's remarkable that nobody hesitated. Nobody said anything much about giving up the normal pursuits of a teenager in high school. Boyfriends. Dates. Proms. She was thirteen.

"I was a loner, I guess. I had one good friend. Otherwise, I don't think I could have left that life so easily and become so completely wrapped up with Herman in a completely new world."

The principal of her junior high school "let me walk out of school on the strength of that letter, written on Herman's stationery, saying he was taking over my education."

And what a remarkable education it was.

In the morning there was a singing lesson, with Herman. Then Italian language and literature with Antonietta Stabile, a diseause who would coach her also in dramatic roles. With Stabile, Roberta did not sing any of the parts. She spoke them. Stabile also had her learn roles of the characters she was playing opposite, so that she would know what they were feeling, thinking. And with each opera she studied the history of the times, to better understand the setting in which the characters lived. By the time she was nineteen, she would know thoroughly twenty operas—and everyone's part, not only hers.

With Elisabeth Schumann's teacher, Leo Rosenek, she studied the German language and German lieder (songs based on poetry). Walter Taussig, who is now assistant conductor at the Metropolitan, coached her in Mozart and Richard Strauss operas. There were ballet, deportment, and French lessons. She worked out in a gym to build up her diaphragm. If she sang arias that required her to move quickly in the action, like "Una voce poco fa," she would practice them while bouncing a medicine ball around the studio.

"I would study with all these people, and then I would come to Herman, and if he liked it, it was a *festival!* Sometimes he would be so thrilled with the singing, with himself, with me, that he would pick me up after a lesson and carry me out. Those were the good days.

"But there were many days when he gave me a very bad report about myself. He didn't like the singing at all.

"I would leave, walk around and around the 91st St. Reservoir, so depressed, so down, thinking it's over, life is finished."

She had serious doubts she could master the material.

"I would say to myself, 'I can't do that.' But always to myself. Not to him. No. Because he was so sure I *could* do it. I had to fight that feeling of incompetence, of insecurity. Whom did I fight it with? Myself! *By* myself. Not even to my mother could I say 'I can't do this.' Because *she* was so sure I could do it. I *had* to! And because I loved opera, and I wanted it badly enough, I conquered that fear of feeling incompetent. Herman gave me the way to do it. You see, he gave me *tremendous* confidence. He instilled that.

"To him there was never any doubt that I would make it. He was *so* sure. He used to say things like, What if you sing for Toscanini? So? He does all the daily functions that all of us do. He brought everything down to a level that I could understand. In the end, I wasn't afraid to sing for anybody."

Except Sol Hurok. Remember, Peerce had listened to Roberta sing again, seven years after the first time. Now it is 1949. Both Herman and Peerce believe Roberta is ready to be heard. Peerce arranges to get the world-famous impresario up to Herman's studio to hear her. She remembers it very well.

"It was a pouring November evening. And I was scared stiff. My voice felt as if it was drying up, and I thought, 'I don't have the breath.' You know, you can study in a studio for many years and be wonderful, but that first step! Peerce was there. Herman was there. My mom. When was my mom not there? I sang the "Mad Scene" from *Hamlet*, "Ombre légère" from *Dinorah*, and "Una voce poco fa," from *Barber of Seville*."

Hurok did not seem impressed. He and Peerce left, and Roberta broke down sobbing. She felt she had never sung as badly.

"To tell you the truth, Herman wasn't too thrilled either. I did not sing well. Period." She smiles. "My mother thought I was wonderful.

"Peerce told me afterward he and Hurok stood out in the rain on the corner, discussing me. Hurok said he'd have to hear me again."

A few weeks later she did sing for Hurok again, at Town Hall, which Hurok had rented for the hour. This time Hurok had all his agents there, about fifty people who sold for him all over the country. Roberta's mother went along, but Herman did not.

"This time I was prepared. I made up my mind it was *never* going to be that way again, the way I felt in Herman's studio when Hurok had come. I was always nervous—and one *is*, the adrenalin has to go up—but at this audition I felt good. I enjoyed it. I sang what I wanted to sing, and I sang things they knew. It was the first really good day that I remember singing for anybody. I bowled them over."

When booking agents applaud, attention must be paid. Events began moving inexorably, the way Herman always knew they would. At the end of January 1950, Hurok set up the first of two auditions at the Metropolitan.

To that one went Roberta, her mother, and Hurok's assistant, Mae Frohman, who cautioned Roberta not to buy a fur coat with her first thousand dollars!

The first surprise was that the audition was held in the Ladies' Parlor. The old lounge had a large vestibule with a grand piano in it.

"It was kind of a studio, but it was still the ladies' powder room!"

Max Rudolph, assistant manager of the Metropolitan, himself accompanied her. The second surprise was that he asked for the trio from the third act of *Rigoletto*, not the "Caro nome" aria. Roberta had been told only to be prepared for *Rigoletto*, so she had naturally worked on the "Caro nome."

"No, I didn't fall apart because I didn't sing that. Herman had instilled in me to be prepared for anything. What Max Rudolph wanted to hear was how fast I was on cueing, my musicianship, how I sang the recitatives—in short, what I knew.

"That audition was terrific. I felt very challenged and very good. Rudolph was impressed, though he wasn't the type who would go overboard. All he said was 'very nice,' but I knew he liked it."

A week later Roberta got a call to come down and sing for Rudolph Bing on the stage of the Met. She wore her lucky outfit—a purple taffeta skirt that her mother had made and a white blouse. Her mother went, as did a young publicist from Hurok's office, Marty Feinstein, who is now head of the Washington Opera. She was to sing the Queen of the Night's second aria from *The Magic Flute*. The Met's upcoming season was to be Bing's first, he had announced *The Magic Flute*, and he was looking for a Queen of the Night.

"It's the most difficult aria practically of any opera. A killer. *Beastly.* Strangely enough, that's all the Queen of the Night has to do. She sings three minutes for one aria, three minutes in the second, and nothing else for two and a half hours. The reason Bing wanted to hear the second aria was because it has high F's repeated. And if you don't make those high Fs in those three minutes, forget it!

"I sang it first in a darkened house. Walter Taussig was accompanying me. Then I heard from the dark, 'Miss Peters, would you mind repeating that?' in Bing's clipped tones. I sang it two, then three times. I couldn't see in the dark, so I didn't know different conductors were coming in from all over the house—Fritz Reiner, Fritz Steidry, Wilfred Pelletier—each time I sang it. The last time, Max Rudolph asked, 'Miss Peters, if you have any high Fs left, would you mind repeating it one more time?'"

In all, she sang the "killer" aria four times, in addition to "Una voce poco fa."

As we know, she got the contract, high Fs intact, starting salary, $150 a week. It was an extraordinary achievement considering she had had no previous experience. That she sang the "killer" aria four times in a row is in itself extraordinary, but she minimizes it.

"You see, one of the reasons Herman was such a wonderful teacher was that F was not the end of my voice. When I studied, I sang Gs and As too, *worked* on G, *worked* on A. So I would toss Fs off like they were nothing. If you feel that F is the end of your voice, you're going to worry, 'Oh, am I going to make it up there? That's the edge of my voice.' But you see, B flat above high C was the edge of my voice in those days."

So *that* explains those high Fs, we murmur. She chuckles.

Let's talk about the debut, we suggest. It was the next turning point in your life, was it not?

"You missed one," she says triumphantly. "It was even more important than the audition, and it happened when I was sixteen."

It was a choice, a fork in the road, one of those might have beens that would have changed the direction of her life had she followed it.

"I was sixteen. I was offered a Broadway show, *Street Scene* by Elmer Rice.

This is a very important thing, because I was offered $1,000 a week! This was 1946! Here both of my parents are working to pay $80 a month for my lessons. The producer came up to Herman's studio and heard me sing. I don't remember what I sang, but I knew right away I didn't want that role. By that time Herman had instilled such a desire, such excitement about this opera career into a little girl who knew nothing, this little *pitzl* from the Bronx—that was all I wanted in my life.

"Peerce was consulted. He said to turn it down. My parents would have liked me to take it, I think. It would have meant some money to them, but they understood. And they, too, were so wrapped up in William Herman, he was like their god. Whatever he told them, they would do."

In the end, it was decided that *Street Scene* was not for Roberta Peters, not even at $1,000 a week.

That does make the Metropolitan debut more powerful, we agree.

"So you still want to hear that old story?" She's teasing.

Yes. It is proof that once in a while, lightning flashes and the gods choose to let a human being beat the odds for a change. A shot of magic to keep the rest of us going.

O.K., she agrees. But first a little background.

After winning the contract with the Metropolitan, it was strongly suggested by management that Miss Peters take advantage of the Katherine Turney Long courses offered in those days. The courses were specifically for young singers just coming into the Met, for extra coaching. They could work on anything coming up in the following season or any operas they particularly wanted to work on. Though she felt a letdown about studying again, she signed up for the courses, keeping in mind her debut, at least, had been scheduled for January 1951 as Queen of the Night.

In November of 1950 she was attending rehearsals of *Don Giovanni* as part of the Turney Long courses.

"There I was with my little light, writing down on my score Zerlina goes there, Don Giovanni goes there, so and so goes there. I don't think many of the other young singers wrote down the different positions of people. I did. I don't know why. I didn't want to come and just sit. Even now when I go to the opera, I picture myself in that person's shoes. Instinctively. As I'm watching, my mind is working, what would I do? I don't want my mind to be turned off when I'm watching somebody else. Anyway I was still learning, still 'soaking up.'"

On the afternoon of November 17, 1950, Roberta was at the doctor's having a metabolism test. One of the secretaries from the Met called and asked if she could please come down quickly. There had been some kind of emergency.

"As soon as I got there, I was ushered into Rudolph Bing's office. He called me Roberta. He told me Nadine Conner, who was singing the role of Zerlina in *Don Giovanni*, had come down with food poisoning and wouldn't be able to sing that night. Could I help them out? Would I be able to sing Zerlina that night?

"I was shocked. As I look back, nothing seemed to faze me. I don't know what kind of a kid I was. I must have been a *horror* at nineteen! But I said yes. I could sing it."

Roberta, ever the realist, talks about her "big break."

"It was good for Bing, and it was good for me. Look, it suited him to have me. Obviously the people at those coaching sessions assured him that I would be able to do it, otherwise he wouldn't have asked me to."

Had other young singers been working on the *Don Giovanni*, taking advantage of the extra coaching? A glimmer of a smirk. "No," she admits.

"Anyway Bing had just had a very unpleasant experience with Helen Traubel and Lauritz Melchior. They were singing pop music, and they were singing in night clubs. He was very, very upset, and he almost didn't want to take them back. So he was looking for a young American to give a chance to. It suited him to have me."

Even so, Roberta. This is your *debut*. Your family, your teacher, *you* have been waiting for this moment for seven years! How did you feel?

"I don't remember! I don't remember," she wails. "I got back to our apartment about 3:00 P.M. (The Peterman family had all moved from the Bronx to Manhattan when Roberta made the Met.)

"NOBODY WAS THERE TO TELL. My mother was working. My father was working. I called Herman up. I'm sure he came over. That time I spent with Herman was very important time because we went over the entire opera together. This was time to solidify. This was the moment we had all been waiting for. Whatever he did, he kept me calm enough so that I would handle it. Listen. I was so primed, you cannot imagine. I was like a racehorse.

"I remember my mother coming in from work at five o'clock. We had been planning to go to the Met that night anyway, as standees. So when she walked in the door I said, 'Mom, we're going to the opera tonight.'

"I know, I know," said Mrs. Peterman.

"Sit down, Mom," warbled her daughter.

"Can you imagine the excitement? My father came home from work then, and he was so thrilled. All those years of working, studying ...

"A little before 7:00 it was time to leave. We went downstairs, couldn't get a taxi! It was still the rush hour. My father was getting blue in the face trying to hail a cab. It was getting late. So we jumped on the subway. I went to my debut on the SUBWAY!"

Backstage, costumes had to be fitted on her. She borrowed "Nadine's this, Munsel's that." She didn't even have shoes of her own.

She remembers nothing about the singing. "I don't ever remember being nervous. I was nervous, obviously. I was NUMB. But I had that tremendous confidence. Herman had instilled in me to be prepared for anything. I had the confidence to be able to get out there and sing it and be sure of myself. I remember being pushed out on stage, and I especially remember Fritz Reiner, the conductor. Normally, he had a very small beat. He was known for that tiny, little beat. But when it was *my* time for a cue, he would raise his arm high over his head and wham! the hand would shoot down. I remember *that* very well."

She was a smash. The critics loved her. The audience loved her. To them, she seemed an overnight success. But as William Herman said afterward, "There was just about as much element of accident in Roberta's success as there is in the meeting of the two sections of a river tunnel, dug out from the New Jersey and Manhattan shores."

Within a month of her debut, she was a guest on the Ed Sullivan show, giving her instant, nationwide television exposure. Her Sullivan appearances would number fifty-four over the years, and she credits that show for making a concert career possible when she wasn't performing at the Met.

And at last she was singing. Critics pronounced her positively "delicious" in soubrette roles in which she played pert, coquettish maids, bent on intrigue— designing Despina in *Cosi Fan Tutte*, hapless Zerlina in *Don Giovanni*, saucy Susanna in *The Marriage of Figaro*. For one thing, the roles called for young, beautiful, desirable women, and for once in opera, she *was* young, beautiful, and desirable.

Her clear, pure voice prompted critics to heights of lyricism: "She poured her notes from a lucid urn of starry "dew." "The purity of sound Miss Peters produced, the loving articulation of the vocal line as well as her easy ascent to the top tones, could give her rank with the Met's best Sophie."

Not only was there the voice. There was the complete control of the material. Herman had prepared her well. For several years after her debut, Roberta Peters was known as the "Firehouse Coloratura," able to step in at the last minute to fill in for ailing stars.

One morning in 1954, Nadine Conner again telephoned in with the news she wouldn't be able to sing. This time it was Susanna in *Figaro*. Roberta had not studied the opera for five years and had never sung it. However, she went blithely home, brushed up on the recitatives with a coach, had a steak before the performance ("If I don't eat, I feel weak"), and went to work.

She was onstage for nearly the entire two-and-a-half-hour performance, never missed a cue, and sang one of the sweetest Susannas the critics said they'd heard.

Another time she was permitted to miss a week's rehearsal in Offenbach's *Tales of Hoffman* because she was note perfect in the role when she reported for duty the first time.

In short, Peters not only made beautiful music, she could deliver it note perfect, on command. She has been doing this for thirty years. Last fall, when she sang her five hundredth performance with the Metropolitan Opera (Norina in *Don Pasquale*), the audience stood and cheered. Thirty years. Five hundred performances at the Metropolitan—to say nothing of thousands of concerts and recitals. In this business, this profession, there are countless cases of singers who flare to prominence for a few years, sing brilliantly, and suddenly are heard no more. Rarely has a soprano been able to sing so long—especially a coloratura. Indeed, critics are quick to point that out whenever Peters' high notes spread, which they do on occasion. Still and all, *thirty years*. How has she been able to do it?

She tucks her legs up under her on the couch, leans close, and chuckles:

"Some people are *greedy*. Some people in my profession sing when they are tired. They accept every engagement. They run around, so that when they get up there to sing, they're tired, the voice starts to shake, they get a tremolo, and then they can't sing. Those are the people who should retire."

Young singers are a different matter.

"I keep telling people this is why I've lasted. Young people today, whatever someone gives them, they'll do. It's so difficult to say no, because the opportunities come so seldom that when one does come you want to make the most of it. You want so much to do it, but it's not always the right thing for you.

"William Herman gave me the knowledge of what was best for me. *You* have to know what *you* can do. That is your only limitation. Other singers will be influenced by events. By people. By managers who say to them, 'Come on, we've got this opening for you. We've been trying to get you something for a long time. We got you *this*.' The singers will be flattered, and they'll rush to learn it, and they may not sing it well. It may be too heavy for them, so they scream and they hurt their voices. To varying degrees, this is what happens.

"I do not push my voice. That's why I've lasted. I've added to my repertoire, but oh, so slowly."

It took her years—until 1974—to do *La Traviata*, which is on the lower edge of the coloratura's range.

"I would not do it before I was ready. As much as I would like to do *Tosca*, I could never do it. My vocal cords are not constructed like that. Managers say, 'Oh you can do *Tosca*.' Never! I want to sing *Salome*. I *love Salome*, but I'll never sing it, not in this life. When I come back in the next one!

"The most I could do of Puccini is *La Bohème* (which she did in 1975), because Puccini is so heavy in the orchestration.

"My voice has matured. The high Fs are still there but I don't have them as easily as I did before. The bottom of my voice has gotten a little bigger. So then some of the top is sacrificed. Now I do Mimi. My voice developed over the years. I could hear it getting bigger, richer, and ready for this Puccini role. And it was a damn good performance!"

On the other hand, there were roles she wanted and did not get.

"There are politics in getting roles. You are asked to do them, and you can refuse, but you very seldom have a choice." Maybe some people do, she muses, but she makes it plain she is not one of them.

There were some difficult times.

"Near the end of the Bing years, the roles I would sing were being given to other people. So I had to evaluate. One has to evaluate one's life at certain times, and you do reach a plateau. I had to take stock."

What she did was actively pursue the other avenues open to her. She might not be getting all the roles at the Met she wanted, but there was summer stock (*Bittersweet*, *The King and I*), operetta, television, concerts, chamber music concerts.

"I can't tell you it didn't bother me not to get those roles, but I wasn't devastated.

"You know, in a singer's life, the times are not all up. Sure you want to throw it all out sometimes, but you don't do it. You fantasize about giving it up, but you fantasize about a lot of things you don't do. In the end, you conquer those feelings of wanting to give up, because you love it.

"I can honestly say I make every performance count. The very best I can do. I don't have that feeling that Eugenia Zukerman has—Sublime in Schenectady. I prepare myself for the performance, I do the best I can, and then it fades from memory, and I'm on to the next one. I don't linger too long on a previous performance."

Does it make you sad that the fleeting moments of music are here so briefly and then are gone forever?

"I never thought of them as being sad. Oh God, there were so many good times. I can't even begin to tell you.

"Singing with Jan Peerce professionally for the first time. Gilda in *Rigoletto*. That was a thrill you cannot believe. You know, years before he had come up to Herman's studio and he was in a good mood and he did the duet from *Rigoletto* with me. And he said, 'Someday, we're going to sing at the Met together.' Beyond my wildest dreams! And sure enough, it came to pass!"

In 1972 she appeared with Moscow's Bolshoi Opera Company. And because of that she was awarded the Bolshoi medal, the first American to receive an honor usually accorded only to Soviet citizens who have been with the opera company for twenty-five years.

And in 1980 she was invited by the People's Republic of China to sing there, the first American opera singer to be so honored. She gave four recitals in three cities—Peking, Shanghai, and Canton—and sang her normal concert fare—songs by Schubert and Mozart—and her "fireworks" arias, which the Chinese had requested. She also included a Chinese folksong as the finale. She had arranged for a young Chinese woman to roughly translate each group of songs for the audience before she sang them, and the universal language of music did the rest. Afterwards, in both Peking and Shanghai, the Chinese audience leaped to its feet and gave her a ten minute standing ovation.

"You know, I think about how music is such an international language and that artists are sometimes the best ambassadors. Singing in China was one of the best times, the special times, I've ever sung.

"Singing at the White House is always a tremendous thrill. That's our *royalty.*"

What are you thinking about when you sing? Especially to the Chinese?

"About getting across the *feeling*, the emotion of the song, so that although the public doesn't know what I'm saying, they get the idea.

"Am I nervous? There's always nervousness at live performances. That's the beauty of them. Anything can happen when you're onstage. Funny things happen. Terrible things happen. You never know what's going to come out. That first note can always be a croak, or some phlegm. In a recital you can start over. With an orchestra, they're going, and you've got to go with them! Nothing ever really happened with me, but I've always had that nightmare that something will!

"I have the fear of forgetting. But I've never forgotten a note. I'm so well prepared, and I know the language. If I ever did forget, I could fake it a little, and it wouldn't be noticeable to the audience.

"But once I'm past the very beginning, once I'm going and I get those first notes out, then I *concentrate*—on what I'm doing, on the audience, on my singing.

"Because when you're out there, there's no William Herman, there's no mother, there's nothing. There are just two little cords down there, two little strings, and your own heart and your own mind."

Once, in Vienna, a usually sophisticated audience of 1,800 operagoers stood and applauded Roberta Peters' remarkable vocal cords, stopping the opera midshow, after an exquisite rendering of "Caro nome" in *Rigoletto*.

Musicians often comment on the instrumental quality of her voice and how it is able to compete brilliantly with the flute or clarinet obligato in an orchestra. She points out that her standard singing exercises included Klose's "Method for Clarinet" and countless books of flute exercises.

Physically, Roberta Peters is small—5 feet, 2 inches; 120 pounds. She is the first to say that she does not have a very "big" voice. But, she says, every seat in the Metropolitan Opera hears her. She has no special method, no formula for projecting her voice over the footlights and out into the house.

"When I'm singing, I don't think, 'Oh I've got to put the voice forward, my tongue has to be down, my tongue has to be up', this nonsense that comes from singing teachers. I take a breath, and if the breath is in the right place and I'm reasonably relaxed, I just open my mouth and sing!

"Herman had an expression: *Appoggiare sulla voce*. That's Italian for 'lean on the voice.' What he would have me do was push the piano with my hands. In pushing the piano away, I free up this whole area (pointing to the diaphragm.) *That* gives me a sense of freedom.

"But there are still insecurities. I am not such a secure person. Even when William Herman was a part of my life. To be an artist there is a certain amount of insecurity. I *must* do it. For whatever reason, I *must* get on that stage and do it."

She laughs. "A psychiatrist could have a field day."

Does there come a time when a singer has to sever the umbilical cord to one's teacher?

"Singers very seldom do that. They become so dependent on their teachers. I was much too dependent on William Herman. He was my life. I was his life. Yes, I was aware of that at the time. When I was having a lesson, three or four pupils could pile up out there before he would come out. He was wonderful to me, and he was not so wonderful. What about those kids sitting in the studio waiting? He lost a lot of pupils because of me. He obviously didn't care. On the other hand, if I didn't depend on him so much, I wouldn't have gotten so much done.

"I see many singers who insist on teachers coming to rehearsals, recording sessions. That's terrible. But it's easier for me to say. I've made the break already. I had to leave Herman, ultimately, because he was opposed to my marriage," she says softly. "I was not taking his advice all the time. I was not coming so often for lessons. He thought my marriage was going to be the end of my life. So I fell off the pedestal that he had put me on. It was a tremendous wrench. We reconciled for a time, but it was never the same. I finally had to stop going to him, seeing him at all. He died of cancer about twelve years ago, a very, very unhappy man.

"I just heard a girl I didn't think was singing well. I didn't know whether it was the teacher's fault or her fault; but I told her 'You are not singing well. You are not singing correctly. Get with another teacher, try somebody else.' You have to try out teachers. She was very upset, and I probably lost this person as a friend. I don't care. Why didn't her teacher tell her she isn't doing such and such correctly?

"Singers do not listen to themselves carefully. I don't think you can really hear yourself sing. You need that extra pair of ears listening to you. The honest ones, the discerning ones, to say, 'Watch it, kid.' The teacher should be the one to have those honest ears.

"If I have anything to say to young singers it's that there are very few good teachers. But you'd better get a good one in your formative years, because if you don't you'll have to undo everything."

We ask the same question of all the artists. Are you satisfied, most of the time, with your singing?

"No! No. Because you go through many stages. We're not machines. I've had many ups and downs in my career and in my personal life that I don't want to go into. There's a lot to a life. When I left Herman, there was tremendous trauma. I had to find myself again. Now I think I am my own artist. I'm reasonably happy with my singing. Especially when I hear what else is around from my era!" There is another Peters' chuckle.

When you hear a young singer who has something special, that makes you sit up, perhaps breathe quickly, what is it likely to be that you'll notice?

"The personality. The aplomb, that imperturbable self-possession, poise. The way they present themselves to you for the very first time, even before they open their mouths. Then, the quality of their voice. The phrasing. The musicianship. It's not fifty percent this, fifty percent that. But above all, they've got to get over the footlights. They have to be able to project their voice, their personality."

She has held a few master classes in her career. Why only a few?

"I'm not a teacher." A long pause.

"Except if I found *one* singer who had the qualities we just discussed. *One* singer who was willing to work. But you see, today everybody wants it right away. They want to get out and sing. They want to give concerts. They don't want to work. They don't even know what the work is. I worked."

She still works. She frequently goes to the Met on what she calls "busman's holidays," to hear how the singers who are doing what she considers "her" roles sound.

"When I prepare for a new work, too, I listen to other people's interpretations. I recently learned a beautiful work of six songs, "Les Nuits d'Été" by Berlioz. There are six or seven recordings out—Leontyne Price, Eleanor Steber, Janet Baker, Regina Crespin (my very favorite). I bought every one. I listened to every note. From all of those, I came out with my own interpretation. It's very helpful. For inflection, for color, for phrasing."

At night, she often can't sleep. Particularly after a performance, she's on a "high" that lasts until three or four in the morning. That's when she says she does her best thinking. She makes notes to herself about what she needs to look at the next day. "A different phrasing may come to me, a different idea.

"There is so much to learn. How can you stop learning? I never want to stop."

During the interviews, Bertram Fields, Roberta's husband of twenty-six years, has appeared from time to time. A real estate executive, he has decided not to fight traffic any longer and is supervising the remodeling of a portion of their home into new offices.

He once said in an interview: "I went into marriage with my eyes open. I understood what she was doing, and I liked what she was doing. Any marriage has its moments of conflict, but Roberta's career is very important to me because I happen to love it. I love the work she does, and I love the kind of artist she is."

Still, it was difficult, especially when the couple's two sons Paul, twenty-five, and Bruce, twenty-three, were babies and Roberta was making concert tours.

"I found it *very* difficult. I thought almost impossible. Except that I had a husband who was so very supportive. I really credit him with the successful bringing up of the boys. They missed me very much during the time I was away. I had a wonderful woman from the time the boys were four and six, but before that, it was a mess. I had a succession of nurses and governesses who were nasty to them, who hit them. My mother was here, my mother-in-law was here, but the house was in an uproar.

"They did miss me tremendously, and I tried not to be away from them for longer than two weeks at a time, but, yes, they had problems as they were growing up. Bert helped them to understand. He helped them to see when I was not feeling well, when I was down, when I was up. My husband has been tremendous. I couldn't have had the career without him."

And what about the boys? What do they think of their mother the singer?

"My sons are terrific guys. We're a close, caring family. But I'll tell you the truth. They aren't crazy about opera." She chuckles. "They come occasionally to hear their old lady sing, but they're not into opera that much."

Paul is working on his Master's degree in Business at American University. Bruce is a Russian language and Economics major, spending his third year in Leningrad.

Roberta Peters, you are fifty-one. You've sung thirty years with the Metropolitan Opera. This year, you'll sing your thirtieth anniversary performance. In 1980 you sang forty-eight concerts. Already you are booked through the 1983 season. Do you ever think about the time when you won't be singing? Does retiring ever cross your mind?

The blue eyes flash.

"I don't think I'll ever really retire unless my voice goes bad. And I don't think my voice is going to go bad for a long time. As long as I know what I can do, and where I am in my life. . . . I'm very happy that I've done as much as I have. All

I want to do now is enjoy it. I'm not a beginner. I'm not young any more. I've worked very hard and now I've reached a point where I *can* enjoy my work and the fruits of it.

"You know, every time I get ready to sing is a high time for me." She leans forward, her hands spread. "I wish I had a nickel for every time I've done "Caro nome," and every time I do it I get excited. It's a tremendous high. Everybody says I give the public so much. NONSENSE. I do it as much for me as I do it for the public. I need it for myself. I'm singing because that's what I have to do with my life. Thank God, I'm well enough. I just want to continue."

5

Mary McCarthy

She wrote recently, "For both writer and reader, the novel is a lonely, physically inactive affair. Only the imagination races."

Yes, and there's the *fun*! In what other medium is the spectator invited to enter the mind of another human being? Novelists *want* to tell us their secrets, *want* to tell us what they know of life, what they imagine it can be. All of their pasts go into their novels—their educations, their states of mind, their heart and soul. Even what is left out is an indication of what they think is important.

The best novelists are like close friends: They alone can tell you what's wrong with you (or the world), and you don't mind somehow—at least for long. No wonder we feel an intimacy with novelists we trust. How many of our friends always tell us the truth? How many of them don't try to con us a little?

For me, Mary McCarthy has been one of those novelist friends. Though I might not like what she says, she tells the truth. These days, that's important to me. It was important in the early 1960s, when I read her novel *The Group*. I, who had grown up in the cloistered 1950s, gasped. There, in delicious, juicy detail were what lay ahead for me—career, love, marriage, sex, children, and not, I blushed to learn, in that chaste order.

She touched with precision so many of my experiences I did not doubt that she *knew*. All other ramifications of that novel—the shaky premise of "progress," the author's disdain for certain tides of thought that swept over America from the Roosevelt to the Eisenhower years, her satirical treatment of the characters—all this went over my head. All I knew was that I recognized myself in *The Group*.

By 1971, when her novel *Birds of America* was published, I had married and had children. My concerns, which once lay in the dubious realm of self-fulfillment, had switched to the war in Vietnam, the environment, and the loss of individual equality, ironically, in a world where individuals supposedly were seeking it. Splendidly, so had hers, and she told me about them in such a way that I could understand what I thought.

In the intervening years, I met her five other novels, and came across her nine volumes of nonfiction—everything from criticism to reportage on Vietnam and Watergate, travel, and essays. I found that Mary McCarthy not only had opinions on everything—more important, she had ideas, and she wrote about both in a lucid, graceful prose, the likes of which is fast becoming extinct in the English language.

It is to her novels, though, that I find myself often returning. That, and because she thinks of herself primarily as a novelist, is why we visit her in Maine—to talk about the novel, her conception of it, the writing of it, its joys and limitations.

A word about plot, before we begin. Critics have always pointed out that plots are thin in McCarthy novels, as though plot were all. Well, says Mary McCarthy in her latest book, "Ideas are utilitarian. They have a purpose. They are formed in consciousness with a regulatory aim which is to gain control of the swarming minutiae of experience, give them order and direction."

One must, I think, accept *that* idea of ideas if one is to read Mary McCarthy—that we live by ideas, whether we know it or not, and if we understand what we live by, we understand, perhaps imperfectly, what we are doing on earth and what is possible and not.

She is sixty-nine now. The once black hair is mostly white. Her face, nearly unlined, is to me quite beautiful; smiles frequently flash across it while she speaks. When she laughs, her hazel eyes crinkle up and almost close.

She had been ill for several months, and though she is now recovering, she walks slowly and carefully. She is gracious, insists on tea before talk. We sip, thus acknowledging the basic civility of human discourse.

Throughout our conversations, she calls out from time to time, to check on activities of her household. She notices states of comfort, inquires about plane departures and arrivals, and listens closely to the answers.

Her home, which she and her husband, James West, bought thirteen years ago, is a stunning example of Federalist architecture, built in 1805. It is in a quiet Maine town, on the main street. Vases of brilliant marigolds and zinnias from the

garden brighten the rooms. Half the year, the Wests live here in Maine; the other half, now that James West has retired from the Organization for Economic Cooperation and Development, in Paris, his previous station.

Before we begin the interview, a neighbor, who is a poet, drops by to discuss the meaning of a phrase that the Wests' houseguest had been seeking. It seems appropriate. Where most neighbors lend cups of sugar, lawnmowers, rakes, Mary McCarthy lends and borrows words and definitions. After all, words are her tools. Incidentally, she uses only the best for her meanings. Let the reader beware!

When I knew her better, I asked if she enjoyed making her readers run to the dictionary.

"Ha, ha," she had chuckled. "No. I don't do that on purpose. I'm unaware of it. I hear about it from readers who make jokes like 'Do you want to give a copy of the *Oxford Dictionary* with each volume?' But I'm unaware of it."

You really are? You really think we know all those words? I had persisted. I had in mind *hagiolatrous*, which had infuriated me as I bumped into it in one of her books.

"Yes, I do," she had insisted. "One of my problems as a college teacher was always that I couldn't realize that anybody knew any less than I did!" We had laughed merrily, but all that was when I knew her better.

Today I ask, when you, Mary McCarthy, are excited about a novel, can't put it down, breathe to yourself "This is a *good* one," what about it excites you?

The answer is instantaneous. "The way it's written. I don't like the word style very much. But the *way* it's written, when the whole nature of it is right there. Just as what an artist does is right there in the line he draws.

"There are all these other remarkable things that you may get excited about in a novel too—some perception, understanding of the character, even some remarkably intelligently managed plot. But those, I think, are secondary rewards.

"I've got this new book on the novel out [*Ideas and the Novel*]. For it, I re-read Stendhal, particularly *The Red and the Black*, and with a quickened appreciation simply for the way it is said, the way it's *written*.

"Such marvelous compression from the very beginning, and how much is got into the crucial chapter—I think it's the third. Everything you need to know and is essential, and at the same time quite amusing, is all got into something like two and a half, three pages. And there it is. The whole history of *Julien!*" She beams.

You wrote once, "The writer, if he has any ability, is looking for the revealing detail that will sum up the picture for the reader, in a flash of recognition." With you, is that intuitive, or must you really search for those details?

"Intuitive. Yet there is a principle of search behind it. It wouldn't come if you weren't looking for it. But it isn't as if you take eighteen possibilities and finally choose the nineteenth. I think just one finally appears, wearing its feathers."

Do you have a sense of wonder at where these telling details come from?

"Yes—but that's part of the *interest* of the whole thing!"

Are there techniques of journalism that the novel should use? Objectivity without judgmental input?

"There isn't any such thing, of course. Even journalists are not objective, and the good ones know they're not. You have to want to be as objective as you're capable of being to do regular journalistic work; but you also must *know* that you are not capable of total objectivity.

"The journalist can't put all details in. He chooses. I think one fault in certain novelists is that they are *too* journalistic, too current. That is, they are too much bent on representing what is the style at a certain moment. I think that's one of my own faults at times, and I can see it sometimes in other people. There's a very hazy borderline with detail, between too much detail, where it becomes journalistic, and too little, where it becomes vague. Gossamery."

I don't want this to be one of those pseudoprofound questions, but I can't think of another way to ask it. What is the reason for a novel? Why do *you* write novels?

Again, there is no hesitation in the answer.

"It's to make something that wasn't there before. To make an object as I might be moved to make some kind of object out of twigs and grass," Her eyes dance.

A novel is more than twigs and grass. I protest.

"The reason for writing a novel, rather than writing an essay or reportage or any of these other critical pieces, is purely to make something that wasn't there before. Something that will then be there, as part of the world of objects, created by nature or God or man, that is semipermanent. I think it's some impulse like that."

You never, then, in low times, ever say to yourself, 'What good is a novel?'

"No, because if you don't look at it in terms of utility, then you don't ask what good is it."

I ask her about bad novels, and she tells me she doesn't read any she doesn't expect to like. It makes a lot of sense and saves time.

What about the motive writers once seem to have had for writing novels— that of expressing a philosophy of life. Isn't that one of yours?

"In some of my fiction it certainly was *a* motive. *Birds of America* and *The Group*. But I don't think it was the primary motive for my choosing to put it in the form of a novel. Or to write a novel. There are other ways of expressing that [philosophy]. But it was certainly part of the motive."

How do your novels start with you? (In her life she has written seven, plus one that is often called a novel by critics but which she calls a "philosophical tale"—(*The Oasis*.)

She smiles at the question, probably because her novels do not come easily or quickly. There was a span of eleven years between the start and completion of *The Group*. *Birds of America* kept stopping because of the war in Vietnam: in the end it took nearly seven years. And her first novel, (*The Company She Keeps*) was not going to be a novel at all but began as a short story.

"I called it a novel. It was sort of a novel." She laughs. "And the publishers wanted to call it that, and so I was perfectly happy to do so. The stories *were* all connected, but they started out as separate stories. Then I saw the possibility of making a connective narrative out of them, with a certain play between "she" and "you" and "I" as the chief character. (In each story the heroine was written from a different point of view.)

A lot of the critics didn't call it a novel either, and they either hailed the writing as brilliant or damned it as "high grade, back fence gossip," but they didn't ignore the first published fiction of Mary McCarthy.

The writing of that book, interestingly, was not the culmination of any long-time desire to write fiction. Mary McCarthy, up to the age of twenty-six, believed she had no "gift" for creative writing. Her teachers at Vassar had told her that.

"Oh, when I was about sixteen, I tried to write a novel in school. I don't think I called it a novel; it was probably a long story. A romance. Later on, the first things I wrote smelled quite strongly of Henry James. I wasn't aware of any imitation, but reading them later on I could see. I'd been reading a lot of James. It wasn't even with great admiration, but he's very catching.

"Anyway, at Vassar, I was discouraged by my teachers, who told me that I had no creative gift. That I had a very strong critical gift. And I accepted that."

You didn't say to yourself, "They may say that, but *I* know differently?"

"No. I accepted that. For a number of years."

Until she married Edmund Wilson, the noted author and critic, in 1938.

"It was Edmund, who, one week after our marriage, said to me 'I think you've got some creative talent. Talent for fiction.' And so he put me in a little room and shut the door. He didn't lock it," she laughs, "and he said, 'Now why don't you sit down and write something?' So I did, and that's all, and it was immediately published."

Lest there be a writer out there, reading this, who is ready to slit her throat, a little clarification is in order. Mary McCarthy had been writing since her graduation from Vassar (Phi Beta Kappa). Not fiction, but book reviews and theatre criticism for magazines such as *The Nation*, *The Partisan Review*, and the *New Republic*. For a while she worked as an editor for Covici, Friede, Inc., where she learned to edit manuscripts and to use all the printer's signs, which were "invaluable." She was not paid; at the beginning, for her theatre reviews. "Oh, something like $3, but it was a very, very small amount of money."

Could you support yourself as a writer when you were beginning?

"You mean before I was writing novels? No. I had a little inherited income, not very much, and of course I was married. In other words, I wasn't totally responsible for my support. No, I couldn't have. Before I married Edmund I had the job at Covici, so that between those things I could support myself."

After *The Company She Keeps*, were there any rejection slips?

"I don't think I had anything that got *total* rejection. I would eventually sell it somewhere.

"The thing is that I learned to write, first in school, then in college, and then doing reviews and theatre criticism, so that I knew how to express myself.

"Actually, you do learn quite a bit about building suspense in a short book review, even, so that my experience finally caught up with my technique."

I ask her to tell me about how the series of five articles, known as the "bloodbath of 1935," came about in *The Nation*. She had written the articles to criticize the leading critics of her day and talks about them with great glee, as though they had been done only last week.

"Maybe I was twenty-two, or still twenty-one. I was very young, and I had done a few rather sharp reviews. Actually, it was Charles Angoff, later editor of *The American Mercury*, who had the idea of turning me loose on those critics, who were really ripe for it. Oh, and they *deserved* whatever anybody gave them." She grins with remembered pleasure.

"Everything was being praised. The most awful trash was being praised and others exalted. You couldn't tell what was a truly great book from a truly mediocre book.

"Anyway, Angoff and I had lunch, and he suggested my doing this. I said, 'That sounds like fun. I'd like to.' Naturally, it was a chance to *star*!

"Though *The Nation* wanted me to do the articles, with the usual mistrust of young people, they wanted a "mature" person on the articles, too. They felt they needed an older head. So they put the assistant book editor on the articles with me.

"Her name is on all of them. We divided the research. But when it came to the writing, she developed a writer's block. In the end, she did half of one of the articles, the one on the *New York Times*. And she asked me not to have her signature taken off those articles. It was very important to her status on the magazine. Naturally, I said yes."

Did that hurt? Wouldn't you have rather done them all alone?

"I would rather have done them all. And I would rather have done all the research, too, because if you don't do your own research, you don't know what you might have found. They paid me extra, but that's how it came out."

Do you believe there are born writers?

"Yes!" Emphatically.

You don't believe, then, that novelists are born in the classroom?

"No. Certainly not. A lot of them have never gotten through college. It seems to be rather normal *not* to have gone to college.

"I think one reason you can't teach writing—and certainly not novel writing—is that young people haven't had enough experience. They might have enough to write a short story, but they haven't had enough *worldly* experience. You have to have, for a real novel, quite a bit of worldly experience; know how people behave, how different kinds of people behave; develop a certain amount of judgment.

"You don't need that for lyric poetry or even for some other poetry. Nor for tales, or romances, or some kinds of short stories.

"I took all those damn things in college myself. I wasted months in things called narrative writing and playwriting. I would have been better off taking something where you actually *learned* something, even economics, than taking narrative writing.

"We all wrote these extremely boring little stories in that course. Then, to be democratic, you have to sit around reading and criticizing the other ones' writings, which are even more boring to you than your own. It's an absolute time waster! And could convince anybody that he didn't have *any* talent for writing fiction.

"There are certain techniques that you can learn with poetry—how, for example to write iambic pentameter in verse. But with novel writing, it's a question of experience. You don't have enough experience to write about, you don't have enough distance from your childhood. For there always is a certain well of experience there that's to be drawn on later. But I think you don't have quite enough distance from that when you are eighteen."

Mary McCarthy did not have enough distance from her own childhood to write about it until she was thirty-three (*Memories of a Catholic Girlhood*)—no doubt because the memories of it were so bitter and traumatic.

At six, she and three younger brothers were suddenly orphaned when their parents died in a flu epidemic. The children were sent, abruptly, to live with strangers, a distant aunt and uncle who beat the children both physically and spiritually. Mary, at eight, was beaten by the uncle when she won a state essay contest—to ensure that she would not become "stuck up." Conditions were so terrible that Mary's younger brother, Kevin McCarthy (the actor), tried repeatedly to run away *to* an orphanage in hopes of escaping that miserable pair.

Finally, when Mary was eleven, she was taken into the care of her maternal grandparents, who had not been aware of the situation. The boys were taken by the other side of the family. In Seattle and Tacoma, she received an excellent education, first at Forest Ridge Convent and then at Annie Wright Seminary, where she was class valedictorian. She graduated from Vassar in 1933.

Memories of a Catholic Girlhood is a chilling, compelling book, because though it throbs with truth and a great deal of pain, it is written coldly, dispassionately. After each chapter, an italicized portion criticizes what has gone before and examines it for accuracy. It is as though the author has stepped outside her writing to criticize what she has written. Why did she use that technique?

"The italic stuff was written much later, when I came to put the stories together, to make a volume. First I had just done them, one by one, and sold them mostly to *The New Yorker*. One or two went somewhere else. Then I decided to put them together in a volume, and doing that I became aware of how far they were from the truth, really.

"I don't mean that they were lies, either, but they were obeying certain conventions that were more like the conventions of fiction. And that's true of all *New Yorker* memoirs: The writer purports to be able to remember, verbatim, conversations which, of course, he couldn't remember.

"And then also, I began thinking about a number of these episodes, and I talked with Kevin, the oldest of my brothers, and also one of my other brothers, about these events in that household. And we were really trying to reconstruct, just get at the truth, as close as we could, with combining our memories. And I hadn't had any help of that kind when I was just writing them for *The New Yorker*. The idea was to have a kind of critique and the thing itself, at the same time."

I tell her that I think she is constitutionally unable to lie.

"Oh, that's not *true*," she cries, her voice rising for the first time that day. In your writing, I say, to clarify.

"Not in my writing," she agrees. "I don't *think* so. I try. I try. I've written somewhere that I was such a problem liar when I was a child, that when I finally escaped from this environment, this horrible household that made me a problem liar, something about the joy of getting out of that and knowing that there was nothing making me lie all the time, anymore, that I've rejoiced in the freedom from it ever since."

Once, in an article, you wrote that "a story that you didn't learn something from while you were writing it, did not illuminate something for you is dead, finished before it's started."

"Oh, that I know."

And: "In any work that is truly creative, I believe the writer cannot be omniscient in advance about the effects that he proposes to produce. The suspense in a novel is not only in the reader, but in the novelist himself, who is intensely curious about what will happen to the hero." It seems to me that you are writing as much for Mary McCarthy as for the reader.

"I think every writer must be. There may be some didactic writers who don't have this view. But if you're writing something, even nonfiction (though to a lesser extent), simply to copy out some idea that's already in your head, what's the point?

"The *discovery*. That's the whole pleasure. Both in small things, just the amusement of putting certain things together and the illumination there, and also the slightly larger illuminations that you get along the way.

"I always ask myself questions, in pencil, pen, or on the typewriter, at a certain point, early, after the first chapter and usually again after the second and maybe the third.

"'What is this all about? What are you talking about?' And I'm usually not sure. I put forward various hypotheses. 'Maybe it's *this*.' It usually comes to me— at least the key, the little germ idea, the seed—in one piece. It isn't a general idea, it's a single image, usually, or a cluster of images.

"*Birds of America* began with something that appears much later in the written book. It was a young man in an Italian hotel room, sort of like a runner. And he's at his door, listening at the corridor to hear when the toilet door will open, to make a run for it while it's unoccupied.

"I wrote paragraphs about that young man. Why it was in a Roman hotel room, I don't know. It all just appeared to me, like that. He was young, he was nineteen, which was Peter's [the main character] age. All that was there. It had something to do with equality, which is basically what's behind *Birds of America*.

"You start with something like that, because it's alive. And you don't question what that means. It's like a little germ culture you put on glass, and then it starts developing. It's only after you've written a chapter that's sort of sprung out of it that you begin to know what it means. You *have* to know before you can get much further. As it turned out, those paragraphs didn't enter the book until Chapter 4. But I always knew they were there and were coming.

"As for general ideas in one's work, I'm sure I don't know about some ideas in my work that other people must be able to see and that I'm not able to. About twenty years after I'd started writing, somebody told me that all my novels were about the idea of justice. I think that's true. But *I* had not thought of it. Nobody is going to sit down and say a thing like that to himself, when he's starting to write something."

Of all her books, *Birds of America* is my favorite. It is about a young man growing up, trying desperately to reconcile the world as it *is* with the world he idealizes. It is a familiar tale of loss of innocence, but with the McCarthy wit, perceptions, and perspective, it becomes fresh and alive.

How long did you carry that "seed" of *Birds of America* inside you before you began writing?

"Maybe I could actually answer that. There was a boy we knew in Paris. He was the son of people of my generation, academics, whom we knew very slightly. He used to come around and see us. He had this terrible apartment. I never was in it, but I heard his descriptions of it, and I can well imagine what that room was like, how dark it was. And he bought a plant. And he used to take"—she laughs with delight—"this plant for WALKS, and that was really the germ of the book.

"That was about 1962, two years before I began writing it. But the idea of equality had been kicking around for a long, long time."

She said that of her novels, *Birds of America* was her favorite also. (She also likes *Catholic Girlhood, Cannibals and Missionaries, The Oasis,* and *The Company She Keeps.*)

Is it your best novel?

She seems surprised by the question and takes awhile to answer.

"I don't know. I really don't think the author is the best judge. I can judge them negatively, but not positively. I just know the ones I *like* best.

"*Birds of America* amuses me, and more than that. I like the hero. I like the idea, the ideas. Well, it's close to my heart."

Could you have written that book if you had not had a son? (She and Edmund Wilson had one son, Reuel, who was twenty-six at the time she began writing *Birds*.)

"No. And I couldn't have done it for a girl. I absolutely don't know why, but I couldn't have imagined a heroine of that age, of that generation."

Mary McCarthy abruptly stopped writing *Birds of America* during the Vietnam war, to which she and her husband, James West, were deeply opposed. It would be nearly five years before she would resume steady work on it.

Those five years were difficult for her and her husband. Their young marriage (they had been married in 1961, she for the fourth time) would undergo one of those rare tests of fire that few of us ever experience in marriage, much less in ourselves. As an intellectual, as a writer, as a "name" long associated with liberal ideas, Mary McCarthy was urgently examining possible avenues of protest to the war. Jim West, though he too opposed the war, was a foreign service officer on loan from the U. S. government to an international organization situated in Paris, where they lived. He had been in government service most of his adult life. For him to publicly oppose the war would be tremendously difficult.

Early in 1966, Robert Silvers of the *New York Review of Books* asked Mary to go to Vietnam to do a series of articles against the war, for the magazine. She and Jim sat down to discuss it. Jim felt that if she went, he would have to hand in his resignation to the State Department. And it was not just his career. He had three children and alimony responsibilities to consider. Mary wrote in the preface to *The Seventeenth Degree*, "There it was. I could not invest his life in my desire to go to Vietnam." She told Silvers no.

Three quarters of a year passed. Absolutely nothing changed regarding U.S. policy. Bombings continued in the North. The war loomed larger than ever. Silvers again asked Mary to do the articles.

One morning in January of 1967, Jim called Mary and asked her to meet him for coffee at the Deux Magots in Paris. She wrote: "I knew he had come across town to say yes."

She asked if he were going to resign. "Hell, no," Jim West had replied. "They'll have to fire me." (They did not.)

Mary wept.

Soon after, she visited Vietnam and Hanoi and wrote two pamphlets harshly critical of the U.S. role in Vietnam. To her dismay—and her publisher's—the *Vietnam* and *Hanoi* pamphlets were virtually ignored by reviewers. Though John Steinbeck, who was pro-war, and Martha Gellhorn had gone to Vietnam before her, hers was an important, eloquent voice of protest in this country, and it should have been heard.

Perhaps the pamphlet format was to blame. The books were purposely meant to be neither hardcover (too expensive for wide distribution) or paperback (too little chance of being reviewed). The long, narrow shape of the pamphlets might have been a mistake too; they didn't fit in normal paperback racks, and clerks didn't know what to do with them.

To this day, Mary McCarthy has no idea for sure what happened to the reviews.

"It *was* a terrible blow, and I will never understand it. My publishers have never understood it.

"*Vietnam*, the first one, was in a way more controversial, and there was more argument in it addressed to our government than *Hanoi*. It's a fact that the format was unusual, and in this country—I hate to talk against America this way—I gather that if something doesn't fit into the slot, they don't know what to do with it, so they don't do anything.

"It wasn't that they didn't sell at all. They were read to some extent. I know they were. They finally reduced the price and had a student edition. They reached a certain section of the public, but not through normal channels."

I asked her, later, in a letter if she had felt that the novel was not powerful enough as a vehicle of protest. She answered,

The reason I broke off writing *Birds of America* to go to Vietnam was, of course, an itch to act. But that didn't mean that the novel was not powerful enough for me. It was just that it couldn't do what the Vietnam pamphlets did: argue directly against the war. There was also a more complicated reason for breaking off the novel and getting on a plane, which was simply that it seemed wrong to be writing through the person of a nineteen year old American boy when so many of his age group were being killed there, or fleeing to Canada or elsewhere. Unless I had done something concrete myself, I didn't feel I had the right to go on writing about him and his generation.

Does it bother you, still, about the reviews?

"It's sort of stopped. If I think about it, it does."

We change the subject.

You've written eight novels. Has anything lasted, proven true over the years in the writing of them?

"This business of having trouble after chapter one, after chapter two. [In one article, she called it a "crisis of faith."] You mustn't go on at that point. Ask yourself questions, preferably in written form. Try to understand: What are you writing this about? Don't go on until you've done that. Otherwise, it goes right into the sand."

And: "The novel shouldn't, in my belief, proceed from an abstract idea, but from some scene, or moment, that flashes up before your eyes."

A "crisis of faith" occurred with *The Group*, after the third chapter, she says. So she put the manuscript away and didn't finish it until eleven years later. It was published in 1963. It is her only best seller (190,000 copies in hardcover). A movie was made of it; it's a bestseller in Germany to this day; and she doesn't much like it. I ask her why.

"I'm awfully mean to those girls. I stopped writing it about three or four times over those eleven years. I felt that I was just whacking those girls over the head and making them parrot this terrible nonsense. Not that they didn't, in reality, parrot a lot of nonsense, but it seemed to me that they were rather two-dimensional characters and there was a little more to them than I got in. My method prevented it; something like that."

You were hard on Libby, I thought.

"Well, she *is* awful. And she's actually based on more of a combination than any of the other ones. One part of that combination didn't even *go* to Vassar! But she's the kind of girl or woman that I absolutely *detest*.

"The only good thing about *The Group* is that I think it is quite funny." And she laughs, thinking about it.

After that book was such a massive best seller, was it upsetting to you?

"Well, for one thing, it makes people in your field extremely hostile toward you. It does. It promotes a lot of bitchiness and cattiness. I think it's true everywhere, but certainly true in New York. And it makes you look at yourself in a new way. You were quite adjusted to what you were before. My books, I don't think, ever sold more than 16,000 copies, and that was O.K. I mean I could live on the results, then.

"I don't know. I don't greatly admire this society that we live in. So there is a suspicion that there must be something wrong with either you or what you've created if you're a success in it. And it may be an accident or a fluke, that's what you hope. But you wonder." She stares at me for awhile.

Another day we talk about the writing.

Earlier, you mentioned coming across details, rejecting some but seeing the right one, finally, standing there in its feathers. When your writing is going well, is that the fun of it then? Finding the right detail?

A noncommittal uh-*hum*. These uh-hums would surface when it was obvious she didn't agree with what I had said but didn't think it important enough to argue about. For her, *fun*, obviously, is not the best word to describe the act of writing.

She considers this awhile. "Really working out *problems*. I don't mean problems outside, problems on the page. Your own language itself gives you a great many clues as to what you're trying to say. The language you use is, after all, an inherited thing. It's thousands of years old. These words can hold accretion of meanings—some of them not so evident, but slightly hidden and they are why you reject one noun or adjective and take another. In that choice there is some meaning and you may find out something about this meaning in trying to make out why you reject the word 'insistent' and use 'steady', for example."

And when the writing is not going well, what do you do? Do you leave it and come back later, or do you work it out?

"I've always worked it through. *I* can't go on unless I feel tranquil about what's behind me. And it's good to have something steady to walk on, to stand on. So that I go over and over and over, sometimes nineteen versions, variants of one page."

Nineteen, I cry. Give me an example.

"They're *all* alike!" She laughs. "No, not every page. Every novel, yes. But not every page. But it happens quite often, and sometimes it just takes three or four variants. And I can't go on until it's settled.

"And then, I either throw the used ones in the wastebasket, or I keep them as back sheets. Then it's a terrible thing"—more laughter—"to start typing on the wrong side of the page [it looks blank but isn't] and you run into your own rejects! Or, maybe looking for some scratch paper, I get out some of the rejected variants and say, 'Now why did I throw that away? It's *better* than what I've got here!' By this time, I've got so far that I can't get back to the stage where that variant fitted, and so you always have to think that your last impulse was the wisest one. Which is not invariably true, in my opinion. But in writing, you have to think your last opinion is the right one."

If you're sure it's the last one.

"Well, then the next one is the last one."

Do you have to let your writing age—overnight, over a few days, a week—to know if it's really right?

"I usually don't. I usually keep doing these things over and over. Sometimes I think it's finished, and then the next day I look and I say, 'Oh, God, no. This is not it.' Or I may look back the next day and think I was on the wrong track and the third try back was better, let's start that over again. But not more than a day, usually.

"When I finally put a novel together at the end, I do each chapter, piece by piece, one at a time. I don't jump ahead as some people do, go backwards and back and forth. And some begin at the end! Anyway, I begin at the beginning and go to the end. Nevertheless, when I read the whole thing through, I may make some very slight changes, cuts, or additions. Or see that this or that isn't clear enough. But not much, just slight changes."

Is there a lot of nontypewriter thinking about your novels as you work on them?

"Sometimes in bed. Especially as a book gets toward the end, there's a certain amount of night thinking, in terms of the characters. It depends on the book. Some of them can get quite hallucinating.

"I felt that awful chief character in *The Groves of Academe* was speaking during the night. Speaking to me or in me, almost audibly. I think I know why that was so because I was trying to make myself into *him*. That is, use some part of

myself that was like him in order to make him real. And so I was making these ghastly faces. I do that, when I'm composing, make all these faces to imitate the facial expressions of one or another character."

In 1962, in an interview in the *Paris Review*, Mary McCarthy mentioned a problem that bothered her then—the author's voice disappearing in and being completely limited to the voice of her characters. The author cannot say anything that the characters would not say, and a lot of the novelist's energy is consumed in maintaining the characters *in* character. I asked her about the problem in a letter, later on.

The problem I speak of in the *Paris Review* interview is not that of restoring my own voice to that of the characters but of restoring it directly to the novel. That is, not to speak through the characters but directly through one's own voice, as the old authors did, e.g., Fielding, George Eliot, Dickens.

In *Birds of America* my voice probably does come through in Peter but it's not meant to. The case of his mother is a little different. She is somewhat like me and has quite a few of my opinions so such an effect is natural. I think you're mistaken though, about *Cannibals and Missionaries*. What is coming through Henk is definitely not me; there may, however, be something of a Dutch friend of mine in him. As for Sophie, again, no, although it's true that in her journal she expresses ideas I have had on those subjects. In other words, no, I haven't got the author's voice back into my fiction yet except in a couple of short stories that will be reissued by Avon with *Cast a Cold Eye* in paperback.

What about droughts and plateaus in your work? Do you run into them, and what do you do about them?

"Just keep on going. You have to ignore them, even though you're aware of them. If you listen to that kind of music, then you keep postponing and wait for a better period which may never come.

"That's what Trollope did in his principle of writing every day. I don't write every day, but the idea is that, good or bad, you *write*. And if this is your life, and it represents what ability you have, it will come out, more or less on a level with the rest of your work, whatever the absolute standard is. I've never had writer's block or any of that nonsense, no."

When I said I thought too many writers made a fetish out of writing blocks, she added, "They must be real because too many writers talk about writers' blocks. It doesn't mean they're imaginary. It must be some phenomenon that is associated with almost clinical depression and that's it."

Do you expect that reviewers, when they review your books, these days, have standards of criticism against which they judge you?

She grins. "I don't know why I expect that, since the practice seems not to bear it out, but yes, I do."

Does the criticism bother you?

"Oh, I *hate* it. Because, stupidly, I still look forward to reading those reviews. It's not only that you're looking forward to praise, that's certainly good also, but *learning* something which you didn't know before, having some kind of *contact* with some other mind.

"With these reviews, especially the stupid ones, a stupid positive is almost worse. I mean, it *is* because if it's stupid and negative, you can write off the negative because this person is just a *fool*." She laughs. "Whereas, if it's positive and stupid, it gives you pause!"

Is it harmful to be misunderstood?

"Yes!"

You would rather be not read than misunderstood?

"Oh, who can say? I suppose you wouldn't because that would mean there was no possibility of understanding. Whereas with misunderstanding of something that's read, there's always a possibility of correction there. And a new look."

The purpose of criticism is the elucidation of art—

"T.S. Eliot," she interjects.

Yes, and the correction of taste.

"I think that is a *most* snobby little definition."

What is, then, a definition of criticism?

"I hate this sort of Brahmin way of saying it, but elucidation of works of art is a legitimate function—the main function of criticism. But I should think if you elucidate a work of art you don't need to bother about correcting the taste."

Do you think criticism today (as in reviews) fulfills this definition, that is, elucidation of works of art?

"I think this is a very bad period for criticism. The practitioners of it are mostly so illiterate today. As far as reviews go, I always feel that certain reputations *need* deflating. And that should be done by *young* people. Nowadays, it doesn't seem to be done by young people. But the best criticism—in terms of reviewing— is and should be done by them. It's much *peppier*! But in general, as far as criticism goes, we're in a new low period.

"Why? I don't know. Some sort of failure of education. You can't call it overeducation, but it's superficial education. It produces glibness and false authority. At the same time, people are completely losing sight of the ability, the power, the faculty of being able to write!

"I've written and spoken so much about this it sort of *bores* me, but all the *prepositions* are wrong. Prepositions are the joints of language. They're what hold everything together and what express logical relations. And nobody has a clue as to what is the appropriate preposition.

"I corrected something on the phone today for a publisher for a book cover, a reissue of *Groves of Academe*: 'a witty, wicked bestseller *on* intellectual life.' I said that book was not a bestseller. I mean it's just *wrong*. And furthermore, *on* is not actually dead wrong, but it's *vulgar*. And so we finally changed it to 'the famous wicked satire on academic life.' Well, at least it's correct. And it doesn't contain a lie."

Did you ever have any doubts that what you had to say was of any importance? That it was publishable?

"I did earlier. I had started a couple of things. One thing I did when I was married to my first husband was to start a detective story. That was to make money. We were very poor, and I thought maybe I could; I read a lot of detective stories in those days. I got to about Chapter 5, and I hadn't succeeded in killing the victim and so I *stopped*.

"I threw it away, but I think I used bits of it in *The Company She Keeps*.

"I know if I feel I'm writing something that's not of any interest or nobody would want to print it, I stop, rather than go on and send it off."

After her marriage to Wilson, and the birth of their infant son, did she continue writing?

"Edmund was very good about help. He always insisted that we get a nurse for Reuel, even if we couldn't get a housekeeper or cook. And it was a very wise decision. Because I could do those other things; they are not emotionally tiring, you know, cooking and washing dishes or polishing furniture. Since we couldn't get two persons, the nurse was the important one. He was absolutely right because I could really go in my study and shut the door and work a good part of the day, while sort of seeing to running the house and doing the shopping and preparing slightly skeletonlike meals."

Wilson criticized her work, but more as a husband than a critic.

She laughs. "I always show my work to whatever husband it is.

"Edmund was not overly critical. He was always somebody who greatly encouraged younger people's talents. That was one very good side of him. And he often overrated rather than underrated—not when he was reviewing some book that was already out, but when he was interested in some younger person's writing, a relative beginner."

What do you tell young writers who want to know what you think of their work?

"I don't believe in encouraging somebody who I think has no hope, really. But the mixed cases are rather worrisome, whether to encourage them or not. It's quite hard to judge promise in a writer, and I don't think I'm good at it. Somebody like publishers, editors are much better judges of promise.

"I'm a perfectionist, and so I value that in work that's shown me. It's hard for me to rate highly work that is grossly imperfect. I can miss the real talent that's lurking there. Also I tend to overrate something that has marvelously turned phrases, even though the central conception may be weak. And I like wit. I probably tend to overrate witty writers, I mean the young ones now."

The second morning we talked, Iraq had invaded Iran, and we discussed the latest news we had heard.

Here we are, talking about the novel and art, and war is beginning in the world again. Does it ever discourage you that the words of men sometimes mean nothing in the face of all that's going on in the world? Do you ever think about that?

She folded her arms and thought about that. Finally, she said serenely,

"That does not trouble me greatly. I have always been sort of skeptical about people who say, 'Oh there's a war on, this is no time for art.' They are usually those awful Philistines who have no regard for art, anyway.

"It seems to me, historically, art has often been a great consolation in times of troubles. But there can also be times when it seems utterly inappropriate. And then, all right. So it can wait."

I asked her if there is something she wished someone had told her before she became a writer, and she said no. That writing was an ideal career. One was free to move about, to practice it anywhere. And then she added softly,

"You deal with things that are interesting. And often with things that are beautiful."

I told her that up to now, every artist in the book had answered the following question in the same way.

Are you ever completely satisfied with your work?

"I'll answer something different then. YES!"

When you finish your work, you say to yourself, 'This is good. This is *it*.'

"I really do. That doesn't mean I'm right. Afterwards I may look on things rather differently, but no, I think it has to be a bit like God and creation. He looked upon it and it was *good*!"

The grin was pure McCarthy.

THE CONDUCTOR

Sarah Caldwell

Today, they are rehearsing an early scene of Gounod's *Faust*.

Marguerite and Valentin, sister and brother in the opera, soprano and baritone, are working in a small dressing room, into which a piano, a pianist, and a long table have also been crowded.

Sarah Caldwell abruptly enters, filling the remaining space, sits down, and says, "Let's get started."

The singers sing. She interrupts.

"Well, I'm sorry. I think it's too fast," says Sarah.

"O.K." says the pianist, and they do it again.

"Excuse me, this is adagio," says Sarah.

"I don't have that feeling," says someone.

"Well, I *do*," says Sarah. "Let's hear the adagio please."

"That's a triplet there," ventures someone else.

"No," says Sarah.

A little later, the soprano suggests they try out a new phrasing.

"Why not?" says Sarah, amiably.

They try it. Sarah is agreeable only if the structure stays intact.

"It's important to hit it on the downbeat. I don't want it to go off the beat. I would like to keep the rhythms the same."

They sing it again, not quite making the changes.

"I'm sorry. I don't want to change the rhythm, O.K.?" She's testy now.

They sing it again.

She stops them again.

"The hold is on the *last* note."

"*I* changed it," admits the pianist.

"I think it's a bad suggestion. This is typical. We're so used to thinking of French as having hard accents. It does *not*. Mr. Gounod knew more about French than we do."

This time they hold the last note.

At the suggestion of the soprano, she and the baritone exchange high notes; she takes the lower ("I have enough already"), he the higher. Suddenly the passage becomes exquisitely beautiful. At the end, unable to control myself, I applaud.

The soprano breathes, "It's beautiful." She looks at Sarah, who has said nothing. "You don't like it?" the soprano asks, worrying.

"I love it," says Sarah.

Relief pours out in laughter.

But Sarah continues, "We're just singing this like gibberish. Let's organize what's being said here."

You see, she cannot afford to stop and enjoy the moment. There is no letdown, no momentary reward of self-congratulation, because after all, there is an entire opera to think about. And after that there are three others to come in her spring season—*Der Rosenkavalier, Rigoletto, Otello*. And above all and *always*, there is the money to raise.

"Arts organizations exist," she told me the first time we met, "because people *will* them to exist and are *determined* that they are going to exist." She wasn't talking about herself, but she could have been. Substitute the words Sarah Caldwell for "people" and you have, understated, the reason opera has flourished in Boston for the past twenty years.

She wills it to happen. Certainly there are assistants now, helpers, associates, gofers, all manner of right hands, but it is Sarah Caldwell at the helm of the Opera Company of Boston, merging music and singers, orchestra and sets into an experience that Sarah insists be "vital musical theatre," an experience that audiences won't forget.

Opera critics, who keep mental notes of previous productions by which to gauge their reactions, are often flabbergasted by Sarah Caldwell's daring theatrical risks; some of them sniff in horror: "The audience applauded at the *wrong* time!" (You can almost hear the sniff rattling the newsprint.)

Does she care?

"Nope! We are, after all, performing for the audience, and their response or participation is an instinctive one. And it is always a *true* one. There are often places that feel like applause moments, and if people react spontaneously, I think it's *fine.*" She crosses her arms, lowers her head, and dares it to be otherwise.

That's the splendid thing about Sarah Caldwell. You feel, after experiencing one of her productions, that she's done it with you, or somebody like you, in mind. The operas, which she takes on the road under the auspices of her Opera New England company, are for *people's* enjoyment, pure and simple. She refreshingly caters to human beings—husbands and wives, parents with kids, grandparents, *families*—and seems to have removed opera forever from the kid-gloved hands of an elite.

For one thing, whenever possible she does the opera in English.

The wry Sarah grin surfaces.

"It's what we speak here, you know." If a translation isn't available, she'll do her own. She has translated from French, German, and Italian texts.

And her effects! They have become legend and breed awe and outrage:

In *Don Pasquale*, the curtain opens on a doctor's office, so you see him first in long underwear. Later, Don Pasquale drives home in his carriage: the wheels turn furiously (the carriage stays in place), while a panorama of a street in Rome flashes behind on a screen.

The barber in *Barber of Seville* dressed as a red and white barber pole.

Automobiles and riots on stage in *The Ice Break*.

In *Intolleranza*, for a scene of a concentration camp, closed circuit television focuses on the audience; their images are projected on a huge screen, over which are superimposed the bars and barbed wire of a concentration camp. The astonished audience sees themselves behind bars!

Don Quichotte, "accidentally" lashed to a windmill, going round and round to the music.

Strobe lights, lasers, rear projection, soldiers marching off stage, then out the rear doors of the theatre and racing around to reappear once more on stage and resume marching, in the *Damnation of Faust*.

A Boston chef flaming crepes in the banquet scene of *Don Giovanni*.

Children dressed as soldiers and pouring out of the Trojan Horse in *The Trojans*. The scale was so good, the perspective so true that no-one realized they were children. (Sarah *loved* that.)

She did *The Damnation of Faust* with a new character—the author, Berlioz, who appears on stage and directs. The singers, dancers, and even Sarah Caldwell stroll across the stage as they would during rehearsal, and the opera is done as an opera within an opera.

Her surprises extend even to schedules and bookings.

This year she opened *The Vampyre* on October 31, naturally. A few years ago she alternately played two operas of the Orpheus legend concurrently. Gluck's rather serious opera *Orfeo ed Euridice* alternated with Offenbach's comic *Orpheus in the Underworld*—and guess where? At the Orpheum theatre. Critics didn't much like the latter. In it was music borrowed from Victor Herbert; Eurydice crooned "He's Just My Bill" from the top of a piano. Sarah left the orchestra pit in a huff after somebody on stage questioned her tempo. Well, you can't win them all.

Besides, the critics have never mattered much to Sarah.

"If it's someone you respect, you're sorry if he doesn't like what you've done. Critics can influence, *sometimes*, a little bit the reaction of the public, but only to a very small degree. Some of the best things we've done, I've gotten bad reviews.

"Some of them were involved with theatrical presentational techniques that were new and which the audience might have liked but which the critic wasn't quite ready for yet. *Intolleranza* was an interesting example of that."

For that brilliant, dissonant opera, Sarah had to hound the State Department to obtain a visa for the composer, Luigi Nono, an Italian leftist. (Rioting by neo-Nazis had broken out in Germany and Italy when the opera was performed there.) She then pirated the lighting expert from the Czechoslovakian State Opera to set up the Laterna Magika, which creates the effect that actors disappear on stage as if by magic. She and the Opera Company of Boston introduced *Intolleranza* to America in 1964, complete with the audience "behind" barbed wire.

Some loved it. Some hated it. None were bored.

I tell you these things about Sarah Caldwell so you know what we're up against here. She is an original. A bold prime mover who sets spectacle into motion, no matter what she says about collaboration. Without Sarah, none of it would happen.

We first visit her in her home outside Boston. We have driven out with her young assistant director, Lisi Oliver, whom Sarah lured away from the Komische Oper in East Berlin. They will be working this Sunday afternoon on the score for *Faust*; Lisi waits in the other room for the talking to stop so the working can begin.

Sarah comes in, shakes hands, glances at her watch, and asks wearily, "Well, what can I tell you?" There is the distinct impression, which will never change in all the times I've seen and talked with her since, that she does not like talking about opera. Talking about anything, for that matter. Doing is what is important. Talking, without accomplishment, is wasting time.

I have plenty of questions, but for a moment I wonder. What am I looking for? Some affirmation from this dynamo of a woman about faith in one's self and a dream? That is, after all, what she is all about. Twenty-four years ago, with a borrowed $5,000 and some friends as devoted to opera as she was, Sarah founded the Boston Opera Group.

I tell her I have come to talk about magic and not about the brown paper bags of money the magazine articles love to rehash.

There's a spark of interest in her eyes, but still she's wary. The press has always made a great deal over eccentric Sarah, the lady who sometimes has to pay in cash because her checks bounced, the one who falls asleep (they say) on a pile of drapes in the corner of the theatre. The unkempt Sarah, the one who forgets her purse or where she parked her car.

They seem to enjoy making her eccentric, as though that will explain the reason for her successes. But that doesn't jibe with the perfectionist Sarah who rehearses her singers, her lighting technicians, her orchestra for brutal, agonizing hours until she's satisfied. The Sarah who spends years, if necessary, tracking down the original scores of operas so the performance will be as close to the way the composer intended it as possible. Enough of these reports have been substantiated to know they are true.

We sit down. She looks extremely tired this day. She has been in New York for two days to cast *Macbeth*, a play without music, that she is to direct in the coming winter. We sit in the dining room of her futuristic cement house without angles and begin. The light pours in and she covers her eyes, apologizing that they are light sensitive.

You once said, a long time ago, "Opera is everything rolled into one—music, theatre, the dance, color and voices and theatrical illusions. Once in a while, when everything is right, there is a moment of magic. People can live on moments of magic." What was the first magic you felt from opera, the first time you were knocked out by it?

The hand is removed. She smiles. "I remember quite vividly. I was a student at the New England Conservatory of Music. I had a friend who was a singer, and I attended some of the opera classes. They were working on a scene from *Carmen*, not an important scene, but the students singing it were awfully good. They had rehearsed it a long time, and it was really quite marvelous. It was my first taste of how wonderful something like that could be."

It was also the quiet beginning of everything new in her life and all that she would become. Up until 1947, she had been a gifted violin student. Born in Maryville, Missouri, (1928), she had been playing since she was three, giving recitals by the time she was ten. She had finished high school at fourteen, had spent two years at the University of Arkansas, and had come to the New England Conservatory on scholarship eager to continue her violin studies.

"College was going to be the greatest thing. I looked forward so long to *going*.

"I was a lucky little girl. Looking back, going to concerts (her mother was a piano teacher who had studied at Juillard), going to the theatre, going to museums, going to ball games, were all very special treats. But I loved the theatre, and I loved music. It never occurred to me that there could be a way of combining these things. I mean, I had just never *thought* of it."

Even today, she is surprised that she hadn't thought of it before.

She was sixteen. The exciting classes she attended were those of Boris Goldovsky, head of the conservatory's School of Opera. His then revolutionary ideas of producing operas in English and of making opera exciting as theatre were planting seeds that would sprout years later in the Opera Company of Boston. Then, however, Sarah was busy learning. She began auditing more and more opera classes and in the end gave up the violin completely to study conducting and stage direction.

"I got more and more involved in opera. It happened as a gradual and seemingly natural thing." She was the only girl in her conducting classes with

Sarah Caldwell • 97

Boris Goldovsky and later with Serge Koussevitsky at Tanglewood. "They were so hard on the boys in the class. I had a ball."

At Tanglewood, Koussevitsky gave her the opportunity to stage Ralph Vaughan Williams' brilliant twentieth-century opera *Riders to the Sea*, based on Synge's play of Irish peasantry.

The Tanglewood production was so successful that Koussevitsky promptly recommended that Sarah be appointed to the faculty of Tanglewood's new music school, The Berkshire Music Center. She was not yet twenty.

Five years later, Sarah was appointed head of the Opera Workshop Department of Boston University, where she would stay for ten years.

I ask her if the Tanglewood production was the first she had staged.

"Nope. The first opera I staged and conducted was Smetana's *The Bartered Bride*. We put it on in a settlement house in Boston with some very good singers— students at BU, some of whom later went to the Met."

Her mind drifts away, remembering. I ask her how she felt bringing music, singers, sets, and orchestra together that first time.

She looks at me candidly.

"I think it was a combination of being inordinately busy and terrified. I don't think my feelings have changed very radically since that time."

Terror is not a noun I associate with Sarah Caldwell, I tell her.

"But you *have* to live with terror. You have to be alert to the problems and the work to be done or else you're in trouble." She shakes that great head.

Do you ever wake up sweating in the night? I ask.

"No."

It's not terror then. Maybe concern, I suggest.

"It's not terror?" She thinks it over. "No, terror is the more honest word."

Sarah Caldwell has been called a dreamer and a genius by her good friend, Senator Edward Brooke, a former president of the Opera Company of Boston. Someone else has called her the Barnum of the opera. I think of the dreamer appellation and the dream she and a few others had in 1957, even as she was undergoing pangs of terror producing opera. Who among us, if terrified, leaps into a project guaranteed to instill even more terror?

She recalls the beginnings of the Boston Opera Group, which later grew into the Opera Company of Boston. There was no sudden verbalizing of the dream. No specific light bulb in the night: We need an opera company here in Boston.

Indeed, the climate in the city of Boston for a new opera company was anything but hospitable. In fact, the old Boston Opera House would be razed soon after Sarah's first performance. Talk about omens. But here's how it went.

"I was teaching at Boston University," says Sarah. "We had an opportunity to do wonderful, exciting things there."

They put everything on—modern operas like *Life Goes to a Party*; obscure operas like Ibert's *Angélique*, Puccini's *Il Tabarro*; old standards like *Carmen*, *Madame Butterfly*; and even the American premiere of Paul Hindemith's *Mathis der Maler*.

They were having a ball. The trouble was, all the talented singers were graduating into what was almost a nonexistent profession in America at that time. Scores of singers, indeed, were going to Europe, especially to Germany, to pursue a singing career. And there was Sarah, conducting, but always classes, always student productions.

"We had evening classes for people who worked. At one of those was a really gifted student named Charles Forrester. He was in his midthirties and a public relations director by profession. After class, we'd talk about ways of promoting opera and ways of making it develop. Out of those talks came the idea to start a company." Eventually, they hoped, it would become a paying proposition.

And that's how it began. In the beginning there were just the two of them, but over a period of time each approached friends, and those friends went to other friends.

"We developed a committee, and out of the committee we formed a corporation and started out." She says it simply, easily, as though starting an opera company were the most natural thing in the world.

The committee met in Sarah's apartment for six months, working out details. Having had experience with committees, I ask if she ever felt after one of those committee meetings that the opera company would never get off the ground? Did she feel any doubts early on?

She frowns. It is clearly a stupid question. "Certainly I had doubts. I still do. There has *never* been a time when I felt the opera company would continue without any problems, no matter what I did or anyone else did. No arts organization in this country is *that* secure!"

There were plenty of naysayers around Boston, and Sarah heard all the arguments.

"It was difficult for the Boston Symphony to support itself, let alone have an opera company. Besides, we were doing well enough with what the Metropolitan imported to us. You know, there are still people who feel that there are other things more important than the performing arts, and you hear a *lot* from them. People who think you should only support hospitals and libraries or universities. You know, we're not fighting against universities and hospitals. We just feel that we have something to offer too!" Her eyes flash.

The new company (whose assets were about $5,000) was given an opportunity to show what it could do when the Boston Arts Festival asked them to mount an opera for the June 1958 festival. Sarah decided on Offenbach's *Voyage to the Moon*, a musical prediction not long before Sputnik I and the U.S. commitment to a moon landing a few years later.

The Offenbach score was incomplete. Sarah had come across it during her forays to the Boston Public Library, but she improvised and reconstructed.

She had three weeks to cast and rehearse the opera. In that attempt the Boston Opera Group succeeded almost too well. Crowds stood in standing ovation. Critics called it a "masterpiece of whimsey."

Two years later she would take *Voyage* on tour to fourteen cities coast to coast where it would lose $20,000. She even presented it at the White House for

Kennedy and his special guests—Charles Lindbergh, several astronauts, and some NASA people.

But that would be later. Now the Boston Opera Group was riding high with its auspicious beginning. Fund raising seemed easy.

"The first experiences I had in raising money were *very* nice. I thought it would be quite easy to continue." A rueful grin surfaces. "After a while, it was clear to me that the first experiences were the exception rather than the rule."

Sarah remembers 1959. That was the year she and her friends sold eight thousand memberships to the opera for $10 each. There was one problem. The theatre they were using at the time only had 500 seats. It took sixteen performances of *La Bohème* to accommodate all the people who were entitled to see it. $80,000 for sixteen performances did not go far. The company was soon broke again.

For the next five years, Boston Opera Group limited its performances to one time for each opera. You either saw it or you didn't. And there were hair-raising problems. There was never a rehearsal hall. Once, a driver who was delivering a load of costumes from Texas, for *La Traviata*, refused to accept a cashier's check

for $10,000—in fact had never seen one and tore it up on the spot. Sarah had a friend, the owner of the Stop and Shop grocery chain in Boston, who managed to round up $10,000 in cash from his different stores, brought it to the driver in a brown paper bag for safety. That was the origin of the brown paper bag story.

The company played wherever it could.

"We performed first in something we called a little opera house. It was a very small theatre, 500 seats. Then we moved into the Back Bay Theatre, until they tore the building down. And then for a couple of years we played in a variety of houses. The Tufts University gymnasium, the athletic facility at M.I.T. A lot of downtown movie theatres. Then the Orpheum, another movie house, became available. We moved there for about seven or eight years, sharing it off and on with rock groups.

"There were rats in the Orpheum. That was a terrible mess. The other performances, the rock groups, offered popcorn, unfortunately. The downtown Boston area is built over water—it's filled land—and I'm told that the rat population is almost impossible. Exterminators were working day and night. They would drive the rats from one building to the next.

"In the Orpheum we would occasionally look down . . . actually I'm not sure they were *rats*. I think they were mice," she finishes lamely.

Andrew Porter, of *The New Yorker*, remembers the Orpheum not for the animal life, but for the magic. He writes:

There I watched and heard Sarah Caldwell, on a small shallow stage and with an orchestra spilling over into what in this country is also termed the orchestra, work her miracles: produce in *I Capuleti, Benvenuto Cellini*, the uncut 1867 *Don Carlos* and Glinka's *Russlan and Ludmilla*, some of America's most exciting operatic evenings; give the long-awaited American premiere of Roger Sessions' rich noble *Montezuma* . . . The Orpheum was a shabby, not unattractive place. Miss Caldwell learned how to turn some of its limitations to dramatic advantage.

She was also luring some very big names to Boston to sing in her productions—Beverly Sills, Joan Sutherland, Jon Vickers, John Reardon, Donald Gramm.

Beverly Sills remembers the first time Sarah called and asked her to sing. It was about 1961. Sills said yes to Sarah's offer, hung up, and then realized she was seven months pregnant. She called Sarah back to tell her. "Weren't you pregnant five minutes ago?" asked Sarah.

Their friendship began that moment and has lasted twenty years. Beverly Sills is now Director of the New York City Opera, and she and Sarah are now, in effect, competitors. No doubt they will find new ground to break, together and apart.

Joan Sutherland, whose rule is six hours of rehearsal a day are *plenty*, stoically went to twelve when Sarah asked her to. The singers came because there was excitement and emphasis on theatre, challenge and fun, not to mention the element of risk. Sometimes the sets weren't finished because the opera company had run out of money; the opera went on anyway. Sometimes to save money Sarah would recruit dancers from local dancing schools and then call them "townspeople" on the program so they wouldn't have to be paid more (with the dancers' blessing and understanding).

There was a story that Sarah would sneak people in back entrances so they could stand and watch when the opera was sold out. I ask her if it were true.

She grins. "That's the Fire Department's business. I wouldn't have anything to do with that."

These were, above all, the years when eccentric Sarah made the news frequently—with great emphasis on her raids in the night to raise last minute money and tales of forgotten purses and automobiles.

Those closest to her know that she is above all things shrewd. If the eccentric stories helped her opera, what did she care?

Besides, stories of her painstaking, relentless searches for original scores are much better than the eccentric ones. She remembers with a certain amount of pain tracing down the original Moussorgsky score for *Boris Godunov*.

"I made the mistake of announcing that we were going to do it *before* we had the music. I knew it existed; it had been published. I went to England to get it and discovered there was only one copy of the orchestra material, and they wouldn't let us have it!

"I went to East Germany. I have friends working in the Komische Oper, and they called various libraries in the East. I finally found an opera company which had recently done the original version of *Boris*. It had been prepared by a young Russian musicologist for his Ph.D. thesis."

She returned to Boston triumphantly, original score in hand, along with contracts for two singers from the Komische Oper and its wig and makeup expert.

It is always pointed out that Sarah Caldwell more than anyone else tries to do what the composer intended, as though that is unique. I ask her when she had decided on that strict fidelity to a composer's instructions.

"Always. There was *never* a time I did not think it was important. Over the years, musical notation has been very poor. Things were handed down orally, or things were known which were a matter of performance style of the period. So in order to make sense out of what is written down, one has to have a lot of additional knowledge that isn't there, but which we need. That has always fascinated me about music—the attempt to find out what the composer was really after."

Those attempts have led her all over the world. Her glee in the stories of the chase indicates the pleasure with which it is done. She tells about finding the original score of Rameau's *Hippolyte et Aricie*:

"That one was gradual. It involved a certain amount of luck, persuasion, and hard work." She grins.

"In Rameau's time, it was a publishing practice to write only the vocal line, the words, and the bass line. And not fill in the orchestra voices, although these pieces were performed with large orchestras.

"Some time after Rameau's death, another whole generation of French musicians undertook to edit his music and harmonize it according to nineteenth-century practices and to reorchestrate it. So the Rameau that is available to us, for the most part, is really second- or third-hand Rameau.

"We went to France and traced some of the places where his music was actually performed. Since it wasn't published, it seemed to me that the orchestra parts *had* to have been written down for the orchestra to play them." She reasoned that the music might be somewhere at the Paris Opera, and she and a friend set out to look for it.

"We spent an awful lot of time in the basement of the Paris Opera. Suddenly, there it was; the music covered with dust. It had been there for a hundred years! When we found it, no one at the Paris Opera was even aware it was there. We made a score from the parts."

She is smiling as she remembers.

Finding Rameau's music is definitely one of the great pleasures of her life. Not only because she found the score, but because additional research on performance styles was incorporated.

It was a habit of the singers of that period to do a lot of ornamentation and embellishment. Osborne McConathy, the conductor for *Hippolyte*, had spent years collecting material and determining what made French performance at that time uniquely different from Italian and German styles.

So they put it all together—the original score, the authentic theatrical style of presentation—and it was all new. The audiences who saw that opera may have enjoyed it, or not. No matter. To Sarah Caldwell, it was *memorable*, and it was authentic.

Another story comes.

"We're doing *Faust* this season. It was first performed in 1859. Then ten years later it was revised to be done in a larger opera house. [Originally it had been done in a small theatre.] There was quite a bit of music that was cut out. We had the printed text, but we didn't have the music.

"I lectured several years ago to a group of people interested in old books and music, and they happened to have an exhibition of interesting old manuscripts. The *Faust* manuscript was in the exhibition! I had never seen it. None of my colleagues had ever been able to see it. The family decided to sell it to a rare book dealer, but I managed to persuade them to let me look at it.

"You see, I had been quite sure that certain music must have been composed. That certain scenes went in an order in which they are not now published, but that would make sense.

"I was very pleased to see that I was right. The rare book dealer was offering the manuscript for half a million dollars, which, of course, I didn't have. But I kept in touch with the manuscript until it went back to Paris and was sold at auction.

"It disappeared for a while, but then turned up at the Paris Bibliothèque Nationale. It had been purchased to be given to the French library. I kept talking to those people and finally got the rights to perform it. So this year, the Opera Company of Boston will be performing that version for the first time since 1859." She folds her arms in satisfaction.

Had she been horrified to lose the manuscript after she had come so close, before it turned up at the library?

"Nope," she says, matter of factly. "Having seen it, I was relieved. I knew then that what I thought existed did in fact exist." She was confident it would surface. And it did.

No is a word I don't think you accept, I tell her. Do you? If someone says, "That can't be done," what is your reaction?

One eyebrow raises.

"I try very hard to see if there isn't some way to make the things I wish to do possible. Often there *is* some way." She shrugs. "Sometimes there isn't. We waited for years and years to do this *Faust*. We were fortunate. It was a matter of luck, to a great extent. But it was also that we were *looking*. Many, many things we haven't been able to find, we don't know, are not confident of. . . ." Her voice trails off. Only she knows what she can't do.

What I'm trying to isolate, I tell her, is, when you are discouraged, faced with all manner of problems, lack of money, a score that disappears—do you ever get to the point where you want to throw in the towel?

She thinks about it. "No." The voice doesn't drop, the "no" is tentative, thoughtful.

Then what do you say to yourself?

"That's a very difficult question to answer. It's more that you encounter problems that are very interesting problems. And you try to solve them, or you get help in solving them. And you know that if you don't solve them, you may be in serious trouble. That is, I suppose, the continual *prod*."

When she has succeeded where the naysayers have been loudest, is she tempted to turn the knife, to breathe, humanly, "I told you so?"

"Let's say I hope I am gracious in victory."

When she *really* grins, a great dimple appears in her chin, and her eyebrows shoot up.

Are you making music first for Sarah Caldwell or for your audience?

No hesitation. "I would say first for Sarah Caldwell."

When you hear opera, not necessarily the music *you* make, but when you hear an opera that fills your heart, that is special and really moves you, what is it likely to be? The totality of it, a certain singer, an aria, a scene?

"It can be the music, it can be the performance of the music, it can be the combination of the music and theatrical elements. It is most exciting when *every thing* fuses together, but it's certainly possible to be excited and moved by one element."

Do you remember any moments when it all came together? Do they stand out in your mind? (I repeat the "Sublime in Schenectady" story.) She nods.

"That's a statement I appreciate. There are *moments* when everything goes well. But in opera, because it is such a complicated thing, it's not apt to last a whole performance. But there certainly are moments when a performance takes off initially, it's apt to continue that way. Everyone is performing well, and it's quite exciting."

Do you remember a day, a performance when it did happen? Not even a massive time. Just one moment when you thought to yourself, for *this* I'm working!

"What you're describing, I think, is more apt to be an audience reaction. I don't think my mind works that way. I'll tell you why. I'm not trying to be negative, believe me. The performance of opera, conducting opera, requires an enormous amount of alertness and attention. If you let your mind, *for one second*, off the things it should be thinking of—You can be enjoying, and realizing that things are going awfully well. It can be very exciting, but it is a very *dangerous* thing to dwell on that.

"When I'm conducting, I'm thinking about the music. I'm thinking about how to help the people who are playing it. I'm trying to think of the structure of the music and how to present it so that if you've made one crescendo, you want the next to be, perhaps, a bigger one.

"A conductor does not just sit back and just *enjoy*. You're in the process of performing and helping others perform, giving signals to people to play a certain line. On the day I conduct, I just hope I am in very good mental and physical shape, that I'm alert as I can possibly be because when you're conducting you are coordinating a million details at once."

And when it's over?

"Sometimes sadness. Sometimes also relief."

It seems to me, then, the enjoyment or nonenjoyment comes afterwards.

"That's not really true. I don't want to say that one doesn't enjoy the music, but when one is an active participant, one is practicing one's profession. An oboe player may play something very beautiful and may be pleased with the result and very proud of what he's done, but he still has concentrated and had his mind on many things in order to play it that well."

What are your criteria for choosing to do an opera?

"The first and most important is that the music is exciting, the music is wonderful.

"And then one hopes to find a story which is interesting and about an important subject. Most good operas are about important subjects and have some social, political, or humanistic meaning or reflect some concerns which seem to stay with us, throughout all time, unfortunately. Most good theatre works are those that express the human concern at the moment the piece was written. And that's what makes them exciting."

Are you ever completely satisfied with your work?

"No." The eyes drill into mine. There seems to be more coming, but that's all she says.

When an opera fails to live up to your expectation of it, how do you handle that? Do you plan to do it again, differently, or do you say, that's it forever on that one?

"It depends on whether the work itself was not worth doing or whether we have simply failed to do it justice. If it wasn't worth doing, we don't do it again. If we didn't do it well enough, then we'll try to do it again to see if we can make it work."

While we talk, she emphasizes a fact she is adamant about—one that is not generally reported in articles or interviews with her.

She says she does not, *cannot possibly*, do it alone.

At this point in her life (notwithstanding the occasional terror she feels), she says she does not need outside people to reinforce her inner convictions and doubts.

"But I certainly need lots of help. We try to get people who are expert in certain fields. She mentions her set designers, Herbert Senn and Helen Pond, costume designer Ray Diffen; William Fred Scott, who is associate conductor; and Lisi Oliver, her assistant director.

"For *Faust*, which has a number of magical effects, we've gotten the man who designs magic effects for some of the famous magicians to design some for us.

"Opera is a collaborative thing, out of many people's heads. And I think one doesn't belong in opera unless one enjoys the process of collaboration.

"I work with the designers and performers, and we reach a conclusion that this is the way to do something. The chances are that at the moment, no one really remembers whose idea it was in the first place. I mean that seriously. There has been so much discussion that ideas have come from many sources and become meshed. When we finally find the right one, everyone recognizes it. And then we're excited that we've found the right solution. But it is a collaborative process."

Then you do not like the emphasis on Sarah Caldwell?

The dimple surfaces.

"I enjoy the emphasis on Sarah Caldwell. But when you ask me what I personally enjoy most about my work, it's the collaborative process. In our company I don't think we put undue emphasis on Sarah Caldwell. We put emphasis on all the participants. Or try to."

What's the best part of putting on operas? The planning of it, in your head? Rehearsals? The actual performing?

"All three are interesting. Planning is interesting. But I have often, though, experienced imagining that a certain scene would work a certain way and then found that with a crowd of people far more was in it than I imagined. Rehearsal is probably the most interesting part of the process, although when you have time enough to rehearse things properly, and you have gifted people, the performance can be fun. But the greatest fun is the actual process of putting an opera together."

I ask her what is in her mind now, in terms of the coming season.

"We're doing a new *Rosenkavalier*, the new *Faust*, and *Otello*. I would say that I'm thinking of them, each of them. One afternoon I may concentrate on one and the next morning on another. The moment comes when I have to concentrate for several weeks on one. When I'm rehearsing, that's what I'm concentrating on. But the planning procedure happens over a long period of time. Sometimes years. Certainly always months."

She is also having momentary concerns for the operas *Vampyre* and *Hansel and Gretel*, which Opera New England will put on during the fall and winter.

"The latter are being revived, so that the solutions to these productions are pretty well known. It's a matter of re-rehearsing. So that what I'm concerned about now is raising money and productions to come that are *new*."

We talk about money. She says the Opera Company of Boston, which has a budget of about $2.5 million this year, receives only about five percent of its money from the government. If this were Europe, the opera would receive an eighty percent subsidy from government.

You really believe, then, in government funding for the arts?

"I believe in *everybody's* funding for the arts. We need money so desperately."

You don't care where the money comes from?

"Yes, I would care. Money with strings attached one cannot tolerate." Eyes ablaze.

"No strings," she adds for emphasis.

From the beginning Sarah Caldwell (because it is she who chooses the operas they will do) has offered opera lovers a feast. A little bit of the old, some of the new, but always with surprises, new techniques, new ideas.

She is particularly interested in presenting new works by American composers. She gave American audiences the American premiere of Arnold Schoenberg's unfinished *Moses and Aaron*. Winthrop Sargeant (in *The New Yorker*) lauded Sarah Caldwell for managing to produce the work at all, let alone giving it such a magnificent production. And that was in the small Back Bay Theatre.

Of *Moses and Aaron*, Sarah recalls:

"It was an extremely difficult work. It took an enormous amount of time and devotion and energy." She stares hard at me, remembering. "A very, very exciting performance."

She would like to present many more American composers, but it is easier said than done. In June of 1980, she was appointed artistic director of Wolf Trap,

the national park outside of Washington, D.C., devoted to summers of the performing arts. There she had hoped to present the music of American composers. Her reasoning is more pragmatic than patriotic.

She points out that Mozart and Verdi's earlier operas were not as powerful as later ones because they hadn't had the practical experience to see what worked and what didn't. But American composers are not welcome items on major orchestra programs.

"We live in a funny world. There is a great deal of attention focused on the American performer, the American singer, the American conductor. And we like to talk about American arts, but the American *composer* is a forbidden subject. Oh, we can talk about him, and you can give him a birthday celebration when he's eighty, but it's almost impossible today to get an opportunity to conduct the most interesting, the most important American music.

"Why? Because everyone is terrified there will be no audience! They may very well be right. It *is* strange, and I'm sure it will change, but at this moment, the terror on the face of the orchestra manager, when you suggest something that is not Beethoven's Fifth Symphony is something to see." She shakes her head.

She has, using the OCB orchestra, initiated a series of concerts of contemporary music.

"Simply because I'm very eager to hear it, I'm very eager to work with it physically. And there is just no place that I can have that experience. It's music nobody will let you play."

She notes the alarm on my face and smiles.

"Oh, I'm just exaggerating the situation, obviously. There are people who want to do this, and many concerts will feature one new short piece. But I had certain naive expectations when I started planning Wolf Trap. I didn't realize the financial pressures; I didn't realize the initial concerns about attracting an audience. They are legitimate concerns. The National Symphony, which plays at Wolf Trap, is concerned that they have large audiences, and they're afraid they won't get them if they do too much contemporary music. They have to keep the place running.

"I thought it would be important to have small festivals devoted to American composers. I'm still going to win that battle," she states, matter of factly. You have the distinct feeling she will.

In 1978, almost twenty years after the Boston Opera Group began as a committee in Sarah's apartment, years that saw operas put on in a variety of unlikely, unsuitable, make-do halls, the Opera Company of Boston finally found a home. It is slightly shabby, not in the best section of Boston but close to it, and it is magnificent. It is the 2,600 seat Savoy, a house originally built as a combination vaudeville/movie house (designed by Thomas Lamb) in 1927, and which opened with Al Jolson and George M. Cohan on the bill.

No matter that the seats don't match. (Half are beige tweed, the other half red). No matter that some of them are taped to hold the stuffing in. No matter that the magnificent domed ceiling crumbles in places and that the statuary fountains don't work—yet.

Exquisite crystal chandeliers grace the main lobby; marble columns and a rich red and gold decor create a splendid atmosphere. Going in, one is prepared for grand things.

Sarah remembers the "miracle of nine days." A miracle because the house was purchased and partially renovated in order to open with *Tosca* nine days later. No one would have considered it—except Sarah. She makes the process sound reasonable and simple.

"Well, we bought the building and had announced performances of *Tosca*, which we planned to do in another theatre, but we found that the rent was going to be so enormous, so much higher than we had anticipated, that we decided we would just try to do it in our own building, once we had it. The trouble was, the building had been divided into two movie houses—one on the stage with seats— by a concrete wall. It was that wall that had to be knocked out. And we also had to tear out the movie house that was on stage, then restore the stage in order to be able to perform. And we did that in nine days."

She smiles, remembering.

"I sat at a table in the lobby with a telephone, and I got my troops moving." There were air hammers and workers and dust and confusion, and she sat there in the middle of it.

Did you ever have any doubts then that you would open in nine days?

"No, I didn't have any doubts. I knew we'd pull it off somehow. I didn't know *how.*" The head lowers, the eyes raise, the grin surfaces. "Let me say, I was convinced that the performance would take place, whether or not the theatre was finished. And it wasn't finished, but *Tosca was* performed."

The Ladies' Guild had cleaned the windows. M.I.T. had told them how to remove the years of grime from the exquisite chandeliers. Champagne was served on opening night from display cases that still held a remnant of movie fare— Raisinets and Milkduds. Magda Olivero, a sixty-two-year-old soprano, sang *Tosca*, not with sweetness and purity of tone, but with character and strength that seemed somehow appropriate in the beautiful old Savoy.

Sarah has a soft spot for singers and a hard spot for recognizing the realities of a singer's life, no doubt remembering that when she began her career as a conductor of opera there was no place for her to conduct. Similarly, fine opera singers were being prepared for careers that, for the most part, did not exist. There was the Metropolitan, the New York City Opera, and the San Francisco Opera Company. The Lyric Opera in Chicago was just beginning.

Things have changed for singers since the 1950s.

Today, a few have permanent jobs with some sixty to seventy regional opera houses around the country. Most singers, however, still work on a production-to-production basis in order to live. As Sarah said in a *U.S. News and World Report* interview on the state of opera in America:

If you're going to make a living as an opera singer, you generally have to perform with a number of companies, so that your most familiar home is the airport. You have to be able to give nice recitals, sing with symphony orchestras and learn music quickly. You have to be quick and adaptable and awfully good on The Tonight Show. You have to give amusing interviews and have a nice stack of anecdotes so that someone can quote you saying something amusing or outrageous.

The successful performer is ... very bright, very quick, who learns how to make shortcuts, who develops facility. And these undercut more important skills, understanding, for example, and that's sad.

Was it more fun in the old days, I ask her, when there was more hustling to be done?

"No. Because it isn't true that there was more hustling. There is just as much hustling today, and though they're bigger numbers, it's just as much pressure."

She says she'll need about $5 million to renovate the Savoy the way it should be done. The shallow stage must become deeper by about forty feet and that will mean excavating the alley behind the theatre. And once the renovation is done, she wants to buy a smaller theatre, in which to put on baroque operas. Finally, there are all those operas to do that still need doing.

"The literature is so vast that it's impossible for one person in a lifetime to [do more than] scratch the surface!" she says, barely able to conceal her joy.

God forbid, Sarah Caldwell, I say, if something should happen to you: Who would carry on?

She's thought about it. "You must understand. The Opera Company of Boston is growing, just as opera companies are growing all over the country. There are *many* talented people to carry on. My one fear is that this opera company will be taken for granted. Nothing can ever be taken for granted." She glowers.

Several years ago in an interview she said she wondered sometimes about the price she paid for the life she leads. Today I ask if she has any regrets.

She recounts again the splendid people she meets all the time, the magnificent music she works with, the exciting collaborations that make opera what it is.

I point out that she hasn't answered the question. Has it all been worth it?

She stands up.

"That's all I'm going to say."

It's time to work on *Faust*.

7

THE ACTRESS

Julie Harris

I wonder how many people, meeting her for the first time, forget to listen to what she is saying in order to hear her voice. Someone once likened it to pebbles rubbing across soft sand; somebody else called it rough velvet. It is at once intensely familiar and impossible to place.

She says that strangers hearing it in post offices or grocery stores will often turn to ask her if she is who they think she is. Straight faced, she shakes her head no and walks away unrecognized. It's not her face that one recognizes, anyway. It's her voice, living in a hundred different characters.

No doubt you have your own Julie Harris. Some of you will go back to 1950 and remember her as Frankie Addams, the troubled twelve-year old making the tortured journey into adolescence in A *Member of the Wedding*. She was just twenty-four then; it was her first starring role on Broadway.

Or maybe you remember her as that delicious, hedonistic, strumpet Sally Bowles, half-child, half-woman, of *I Am A Camera*. Christopher Isherwood, who wrote the stories on which the play was based, was convinced that Julie was the real life Sally Bowles when he first saw her in costume.

"Isn't it a pity," Isherwood had whispered. "You are still as you were, and I am twenty years older."

To some of you, Julie Harris will always be Joan of Arc, jubilant, radiant, in *The Lark*. For others, Mary Todd Lincoln will leap to mind, weeping in humiliation and rage. Or the forty-year old ravishing divorcée of *Forty Carats*; or Sister Brigid Mary Mangan in *Little Moon of Alban*; or poor Anna in *And Miss Reardon Drinks a Little*; *Mademoiselle Colombe*, or Ophelia, or Juliet; Queen Victoria or Florence Nightingale; Mrs. Pinchwife, or Johnny Belinda; or dozens of parlormaids, actresses, spinsters, queens, dope addicts, sisters, lovers, mothers, or crooks. For all of these there is a Julie Harris whom someone will remember.

For me, and at least one anonymous woman a critic mentioned in a review of *The Belle of Amherst*, Julie Harris is and always will be Emily Dickinson, the maiden poet.

The critic wrote: "When Miss Harris ever so gently glided into 'Because I could not stop for Death, He kindly stopped for me', a sound that was half-gasp, half-sighing approval [came] from a woman seated near me. The lines can only have fallen newly on her ears; the sound she made is one we should be hearing more often in the theatre."

That gasp characterizes the theatre at its best, I think. The gasp of recognition that astonishes and clarifies. In the best of times in the theatre, it does not come often. When it does, Julie Harris is often nearby, evoking it. We met in New York, where she was rehearsing for James Prideaux's new play *Mixed Couples*, and we talked about the gasp and other joys of her work.

It is a splendid Indian summer morning. On the way to her hotel, the cab driver plays a tape for George and me of his own saxophone music, recorded in his home. "You couldn't sell that," he announces. "I do it because I love it, but art don't sell."

His words are ringing in my ears as we shake hands with Julie Harris for the first time and will stay with me all the time we spend with her.

She is not very big, this actress whose presence fills a stage. She's only about 5 feet 4 inches tall. Her hands are small; fine bones mold a delicate face; her eyes are bright blue; she has a redhead's pale complexion; some pale freckles show through.

She wrote me, before we met, that she was reluctant to talk about herself. I replied that it was her work I wanted to talk about. Even so, she isn't sure. Soon after we sit down, she says,

"*All* I am is an actor. A translator. I'm a crucible where the feeling goes in and it's distilled in me, and then you *hope* it goes out to the audience through the play. All we have to give is what we are." She frowns, as though wondering if I understand.

I don't tell her so, but I want to shout, that's it! *That* is art and is what causes gasps.

But instead I ask, Have you ever thought what makes us connect with a character in the theatre? What spark is it that is struck in us, thrown off by the play as it is acted through the characters?

"It's that question—'What are we? What *are* we?'—that makes drama all the time. And the choices we make, that we are always confronted with, *always*, that never end until the grave."

Have you ever experienced that gasp of astonishment that you so often manage to evoke in others?

"Did you ever see Laurette Taylor?" she counters. "*I* did. She was in *The Glass Menagerie*, and I saw her through a blur of tears and laughter. I was only about eighteen or so, and I hadn't lived *that* long, but she made me see everything I had ever felt since I was born! Conflicts with my mother and father. *Everything!* She was so beautiful. So *funny!*"

She leans forward, her face glowing.

"There's an actor who is rehearsing the play *Amadeus* on the same floor that we are. Ian McKellan. I've seen him in two plays in England, and he is *extraordinary*. Watching him is like sunlight pouring in. Everything that he does is clear and moving or funny and reveals something to you of yourself. The critics haven't seen him here; he's never performed in the U.S. But when they do, it will be like discovering a new comet!"

She talks about Geraldine Page, who costars with her in the new play. During rehearsal "part of me is watching Gerry, and the transformation that is taking place in her. It is extraordinary.

"I'm constantly revived by my idols, people I love, actors and actresses and playwrights. To me, the Barrymores and the Lunts were aristocracy, they were the royalty of life. The actors are the princes and princesses."

She thinks a while and then adds softly,

"To me, the theatre is a holy place. I believe it is able to tell us about the spiritual power of God. The playwright, after all, is also trying to tell us some message about living.

"Of course it is corrupted. The theatre has always been pushed around. 'What can you expect?' she intones in a low voice, imitating imagined authority. 'They're *theatre* people.'

"Well, you can say that about almost every aspect of human endeavor, because everything is going to be corrupted and does get corrupted." Her eyes are blazing.

It's the uncorrupted theatre I want to talk about, I say. The one that connects between actor and audience, the one that makes revelations.

"Then it's *glorious*." She settles back, happily.

I've noticed this in talking with Julie Harris for just a few minutes: To be with her is to feel heat, not just warmth; the very air around her vibrates with intensity. Her space throbs with life.

Julie's mother once told her, after an especially moving performance in a school play, "Come on. Snap out of it. It's *only* a play!"

Only a play! That must have pierced Julie's heart—she who says of the theatre, the play is the voice that *must* be heard; who at sixteen answered, "It's my *life!*" when a teacher asked her why she wanted to study drama; who once screamed at an actor who had come late, and slightly inebriated to rehearsal, "We don't *do* that in the theatre!" and refused the flowers he sent in apology.

I ask her what she was like as a girl, growing up.

"I was odd and gawky, and the boys who liked me, *I* didn't like. They were *creeps.*" Her voice lowers. "*Now* they wouldn't be, but *then* they were. I was in love with the football heroes, and they couldn't see me for dust."

Her mother was a nurse, her father an investment banker who had the time and money to pursue his avocation—he was associate curator of mammals at the University of Michigan. Julia Ann and her two brothers lived in an affluent suburb of Detroit—Grosse Pointe. Her mother loved social life, wanted Julie to "come out." Julie refused.

"In those days, growing up in the 1930s and 1940s, we weren't so much looking forward to a career. You saw families around you. You fell in love, and you married and had a family. That was the ultimate.

"Or else you were different, like me. You were odd, and boys didn't like you. So you had to think of something else to do.

"Nursing interested me and even medicine. But I couldn't get through math, so how could I do that? Then my father said, 'You must learn stenotyping,' and I thought I'd rather cut my throat. I didn't want to be a secretary, sit in an office, and take somebody's dictation. Keep files. I *didn't* want to do it. What *could* I do?

"So then there was acting in school, which was fun. I was a good mimic, and I always got the juicy parts in the school plays."

She tells about the first role she played that had emotional depth to it, the juggler in *Le Jongleur de Notre Dame*. She was only about twelve or thirteen.

"How could I forget that? It's a Christmas story, where the juggler is given sanctuary in the church. He is poor and has no money. On Christmas Eve, all the people come from the village to bring gifts to the Virgin, and he has nothing."

She whispers, "So he *juggles*. He does his act for the Virgin and she smiles— and that's the miracle."

Until the night of the performance, Julie did not know what she would do about the juggling. When the time came, she did it in mime. A very old magazine article reports that there were those in the audience with tears in their eyes, but Julie doesn't remember that.

"Only my mother could, and she's gone. I don't know if I cried or if I acted it well. All I remember is that it had an impact on me about how wonderful it was to *be* there, in a story that had some meaning. To be *part* of it and that it moved people. For the first time, it was apparent to me how powerful the theatre could be."

She persuaded her parents, who weren't terribly enthusiastic, to let her study acting during the summer at the Perry/Mansfield Theatre Workshop in Steamboat Springs, Colorado. For three years, she waited on tables all summer in order to save $150 tuition. "Charlotte Perry taught me acting," she says simply.

"And Miss *Hewitt*!" she cries.

Miss Hewitt's classes. Famous in New York, Caroline Hewitt was a kind of queen among headmistresses in that city. Besides running an excellent school, Caroline Hewitt had a wide knowledge and love of the theatre—especially actors. Julie spent her last year of school there, studying drama, and then on graduation Miss Hewitt invited Julie to live with her for a year and a half. What an education that was.

"She was an encouragement all the way through. Oh, God, if I had only had some sense in those days! Her story is a miracle, real Jane Eyre. She started the most exclusive girl's school in New York, the toughest city to crack, this young woman from England with nothing and no education. Just a great spirit and her own sort of fineness. Shakespeare was her god because you couldn't have any better. She instilled that in young girls and the finest of music and art."

Did she ever prepare you for the realities of an actor's life or barren years?

Julie smiles. "She said, 'Be quiet. Be careful of your passion. Your passion is going to undo you!' But that happens with everybody. Passion undoes you, one way or the other. I mean, we're not *machines*!" Julie cries.

In 1944, because she thought she ought to know about the technical operations of the theatre—lighting and set construction—Julie enrolled in the Yale School of Drama for a year.

She auditioned for the Actor's Studio. "It gave me a feeling that I belonged somewhere." She felt a basic distrust in herself. A tendency to rush into something without feeling her way. That feeling would stay with her, though it lessened, all through her life.

During her Yale year, Julie made her first Broadway appearance, as Atlanta in Curt Goetz' play, *It's a Gift*. The play ran six weeks. Her one review said noncommittally, "The daughter was played by Julie Harris."

In 1946 she landed walk-on parts with the visiting Old Vic Company (one of three Americans chosen) and watched Laurence Olivier and Ralph Richardson work. Later, she would remember those times as one of her happiest in theatre. To her, forty weeks of repertory is the ideal: an actress can star in a play one year, then take a supporting role the next. She points out ruefully that even if there were a secondary role she liked, it would not be offered to her because she's starred.

She read for Nelly in *Playboy of the Western World*. When producer Guthrie McClintic turned her down because she didn't look Irish enough, Julie immediately broke down in tears in his office. It's hard to believe that this red-haired, freckled wisp of a woman never looked sufficiently Irish, even as a girl. (She *did* get the part.)

Many theatregoers mark Julie's appearance in *Member of the Wedding* as her Broadway debut, but she points out that she worked quite a bit between *It's a Gift*, in 1945, and 1950. There were eleven roles and don't forget the White Rabbit in *Alice in Wonderland*. She got married, too, to a young lawyer who also produced plays. They lived in a fifth floor walk-up on 58th Street.

"I did, pretty soon, begin to support myself, but I was married, so that when I wasn't working, I had someone taking care of me. A lot of my friends did all kinds of odd jobs, waiting on tables and modeling and being telephone operators." She didn't have to take other jobs to supplement their income, but money was very scarce.

She remembers, one day at home, being talked into buying a magazine subscription by a fast-talking salesman for $13.25. The next day she was at the office in tears pleading for the money back. It was one of her best performances. She got the refund.

In those lean years, did you ever get discouraged? I ask.

"Not too discouraged. Not discouraged enough to give up. I *never* would consider giving up." She glares at me. "Never."

Member of the Wedding was the beginning of everything big for Julie Harris. The critics praised this twenty-four year old who played so convincingly the role of a twelve-year old. Brooks Atkinson, by the intensity of whose reviews one can chart the career of Julie Harris, pronounced her a "very gifted young actress."

The play ran for a year and a half, then went on tour for six weeks. The last night, Julie sobbed her way through the performance. "Ethel (Waters) had to turn me around, set me down, stand me up. She and Brandon de Wilde had been like family to me. I knew I was going into another play the next season and would never do this play again. Never do it again!" The enormity of that she still feels, her face a study in despair.

That fall, she burst onto the stage again as Sally Bowles, the lovable tart of *I Am A Camera*. "No Leica," pronounced one critic about the play, but they all liked Julie. This time, Brooks Atkinson pronounced her a "remarkable actress."

After fifty performances of the play, the producers had a seven foot cutout of Julie Harris as Sally Bowles fastened to the marquee and proclaimed her name in lights above the title. It now read: "Gertrude Macy and Walter Starcke have the pleasure to announce the stardom of Miss Julie Harris."

On seeing it, Julie wept.

For her performance as Sally, Julie won the theatre's most coveted award, a Tony. It would be the first of five.

Next was the title role in *Mademoiselle Colombe*, a saucy French satire that ran only two months. Wrote Atkinson, "Miss Harris is a rare actress. Her Colombe is a masterpiece in miniature."

That fall of 1954 she married stage manager Manning Gurian and began doing research for the biggest role of her life, St. Joan, in Lillian Hellman's adaptation of Jean Anouilh's play *The Lark*. When she learned she was pregnant, she offered to give up the part, but Kermit Bloomgarden, the producer, wanted only her and was willing to wait a year, until after the baby's birth. She wanted that role so badly she offered to take a smaller percentage until the costs were paid off and to go on the road for a flat sum.

For three months after Peter Gurian's birth, Julie took care of her son, nursed him, and studied books on Joan of Arc. The more she read, the more she was terrified. Images of all the great St. Joans—Sarah Bernhardt, Julia Marlowe, Maude Adams, Katharine Cornell, Ingrid Bergman, Uta Hagen—paraded through her mind. As she would do for all her later roles of historic women, Julie devoured volumes on the subject—biographies, letters, the original trial records, anything that would illuminate the character.

Julie Harris' St. Joan was a soaring triumph to critics and to audiences. Brooks Atkinson pronounced her performance "luminous." Walter Kerr said she "devoured" the role. One critic said her growth of the character throughout the play was almost psychic, but she did not, she felt, ever quite meet her own estimation of how to play St. Joan.

In an interview with Brock Brower of the *Saturday Evening Post*, she said, "I didn't always get there. I know that. But if I hadn't tried always to make the effort, that play couldn't have held up."

St. Joan earned her a second Tony.

The Lark ran two hundred and twenty-nine performances and closed June 2, 1956. Before she opened in the comedy *A Shot in the Dark* five years later, she appeared on Broadway in three other plays that ran a total of only one hundred and fifty-two performances. But she worked—a couple of unmemorable movies and some fine television appearances (*Little Moon of Alban*, an unforgettable *Victoria Regina*, a television filming of *The Lark*, *Johnny Belinda*, and *A Doll's House*), though television's very method often turned the magic off.

She always felt inadequate, but television heightened that feeling. She'd spend hours in rehearsal, becoming more and more tense. Finally, in a run through, she would give what she felt, what she *knew* was her best performance, for the cameraman. When the actual telecasting happened, she believed there was only a quarter of herself to give.

In 1961 she was back on Broadway, in *A Shot in the Dark*. In this Parisian comedy, Julie played a bawdy, uninhibited parlormaid. She remembers that play with bittersweet feelings. After a week of rehearsals, Julie begged her husband to get her out of it. She was *sure* she would fail in it. The part demanded that she have so much "good humor and freedom," and her confidence was at a low ebb. But she did not get out of it.

"Donald Cook opened in the play with me in New Haven. The laughter itself was a startling experience, because the whole stage seemed to rock. The audience loved him. But I was upset. Donald said to me after the first runthrough with an audience, 'You're not going to say the lines that fast, are you?' I just tore through it, because I wanted to get all the words out. I was afraid. I was scared."

But the laughter came in great healing waves.

"I remember thinking Donald is *so* brilliant. He was a brilliant comedian. And then he had a heart attack when we were in New Haven. And Donald died."

I am stunned. She has made this man, in gestures and voice, come so alive that I, who had known of his existence only moments before, now grieve for his death.

"What a shock," she whispers. "We lost him, and I thought, well, that's it." She spreads her hands. "But then they got Walter Matthau. He was quite different from Donald, but terribly funny. It was a perfect part, and Walter was wonderful in it. So the play was a success!"

A hit. But the next one was not. For her friend June Havoc's autobiographical play, *Marathon '33*, Julie went to her usual thorough lengths.

The summer of 1963, she studied June Havoc's old dance routines, learned the time step and the clog dance (wearing clogs). She lugged around a weighted dummy to simulate a sleep-drugged partner she'd have to drag around on the stage.

A couple of years earlier, she had lamented in an interview, "I think it's a sad thing New York has come to, hits or no hits. So many good things are lost because they don't make that hit box."

Even Julie's excellent performance did not save *Marathon '33*.

What is it, I ask her, that makes you decide to take a role? What makes you say yes?

She thinks about it. "Some moment in the play. Your ears prick up and you feel tingly and you get *excited*. I know from the first reading if I want to do it." Then she adds candidly, "Sometimes I'll do something for the director. I love to work with good ones." She mentions Charles Nelson Reilly, who directed her in *Belle of Amherst*, and George Schaefer, who is currently directing her in *Mixed Couples*.

Over the years, she has worked with dozens of other directors, the brilliant and the not so brilliant. I ask her how much of what she wants in a role is implemented. Does she fight for her ideas, her interpretations? And how does she make what she feels is important come through, if it's at odds with the director?

She illustrates with an example from the play they're doing now.

"George Schaefer is a fine director. And George is very much like a school teacher. 'No, no,' he says. 'No.' He has a wonderful ear.

"In the play, my character is always saying, 'Nothing matters. Life, what does it matter? Who cares?' That's her attitude on the outside. Then at the end of the play, she says, 'Well, maybe it does matter, maybe I'm all wrong. I can see them now, lowering my coffin into the ground, and they'll hear this voice come out saying, 'Oh my God. It *mattered*."

I roar with laughter at this miniscene, the last words of which she has delivered in a huge throbbing voice.

"Now George says, 'I don't think the audience should laugh at that.' He wants it to be *sad*." She leans forward and whispers,

"Now *I* think it's funny. I don't believe he's right. So we have to work, we have to collaborate. I was using a huge voice coming from the grave. Because it suddenly reminded me of a fairy tale, the teeny tiny lady in the teeny tiny house, and she hears a teeny tiny noise. And it gets bigger until finally she says in a huge voice at the end of the story, WHO IS IT? And the whole house shakes!

"I was recalling that little story to him yesterday, but he said, No, this was the way it's got to be. So I did it then, with a very tiny voice. Now I understand what *he* wants. But I have to get part of what *I* want. So I'm going to do it with a very small voice, but it's going to be very PENETRATING. Maybe that will be a good compromise.

"I always feel that, in this time of working on a play, we should try *everything*. Sometimes you do something and it's all wrong and you find that out. And sometimes you try it and find out *he* could be wrong. It's a sort of blending. So, I've lost my big voice, but maybe this penetrating one with the smaller voice will be more effective."

(P.S. It got laughs. You never know.)

What is the best time for you in a play? The reading of it? The working it out through rehearsal, or the performance?

"It's the working." Then she reconsiders. "The doing it for an audience. No. *All* of it. The rehearsal part is very exciting, but the audience completes it, really makes it come to life, especially in comedy. Comedy is so dazzling. And so *beneficial*."

During rehearsal, when the play starts to glow, to really become alive, do you all feel it at once, or is it a different time for each actor?

"It seems that it happens all at once. We find the scene together, and we all *know* it. We don't discuss it then, because it's an elusive thing. But we say, 'Oh, that feels good.'

"It's just beginning to happen with *Mixed Couples*. You know, plotting it out, doing it, repeating it, and trying to find it in different ways is sometimes just mere *drudgery*—you feel like a *drudge*. Then finally, it starts to come to life, and you're after it then, you know it's there somewhere, and it's very exciting."

Her eyes shine.

Sometime, along about the time Julie Harris was playing in A *Shot in the Dark*, the germ of the most "extraordinary" thing that was ever to happen in her career was beginning, slowly, to grow.

"Caedmon Records asked me to do a recording of the poems and letters of Emily Dickinson. I had not read much of her before, perhaps a few poems in high school. The script came, I read it and thought, 'Well, it's nice to make a record.' I worked with Howard Sackler, who wrote *The Great White Hope*. At that time, he directed all of Caedmon's spoken recordings.

"As I worked with Howard, the letters became very intriguing to me. The language was so odd, the words so powerful because they were so personal. And the humor was *wonderful*." She leans close with that conspiratorial whisper that causes one's interest to surge. "So oblique, and yet very powerful.

"After the record was made, I went to the store and bought some biographies of Emily. Then I bought the letters—three volumes, from the Harvard Press—because something seemed to say to me, 'You've got to read those. That's the best source. That's *her*.' And from then on, I would pick them up and read them from time to time."

Julie is a voracious reader, especially biographies of women. Several times during the interview she stops to recommend books I ought to read, recreating scenes from them that are apropos to our discussion. She especially urges acquaintance with the letters of Dora Carrington, Lytton Strachey's friend, which she hopes to dramatize some day.

Now she spins out the tale of Charlotte Brontë's experience in a Catholic church, confessing a forbidden love. She becomes Charlotte, and I am suddenly in another century, sharing in Charlotte's pain. Abruptly the scene ends, and Julie asks happily,

"Isn't that powerful stuff?"

We resume talking about Emily Dickinson.

"Anyway, my son Peter was about five or six, and in the afternoons he would attend a craft class that was run by a young man whose father was an Episcopal priest. Nick, the young man, had always loved the theatre. One day he said that his father wondered if I would ever be interested in doing something for his church group, as a benefit?

"'What could I do?' I said to Nick. 'I don't do anything solo you know.'

"'There's nothing you can do by yourself?'

"'Well, I could do Emily Dickinson. Would that interest you?' 'Oh, yes, it would.' Then I was *stuck*. I had committed myself to doing this benefit, and it was going to be in a theatre and they were going to sell tickets!

"At first, I was just going to read a few poems. But *you have to do more than that* for an evening," she intones.

"I said, Oh my God. Here I was faced with preparing that program, but I had a summer to do it, and so I went away and I *prepared*.

"I said to myself, I've got to give a portrait of her, it seems to me. I've got to *be* her, wear the costume, a white dress, get a few hand props, and I have to have the letters. I memorized the poems, but I decided to *read* the letters.

"I went through all the books, I collected the poems that I loved and put the thing in chronological order, along with the letters. I had all that typed up. Then, I would rehearse it by myself in my room. It was two hours long."

As you were doing it, did it sound good to you?

She smiles. "When Charlie saw it [Charles Nelson Reilly with whom she had done the musical *Skyscraper*], he came rushing backstage and roared, 'It's GANGBUSTERS! You had me from the time you read Dear Abiah.'"

Did you know it was gangbusters?

"Of course, I knew it," she cries. "I knew Emily was *tremendous*, and doing her had this curious effect on me. Here I was, doing something I had never done before, and I wasn't shaking like an aspen leaf. I was just very happy. I was looking forward to it and thinking now *everybody* is going to hear this. Isn't it wonderful?"

What did the audience think of it?

"From the very first, they wanted to hear more. I mean, Emily *is* a unique voice. You want to stand up and *cheer*!"

And did they stand up and cheer that night?

She smiles. "I *think* so."

The benefit was held at the Booth Theatre in New York, and it was not reviewed. It would be nearly fifteen years before the one woman play *Belle of*

Amherst, written by William Luce, starring Julie Harris, and directed by Charles Nelson Reilly, opened on Broadway. In those fifteen years lies a tale that is common to the theatre—endless waiting, trying, disappointments, trying something new, waiting again. And then sudden, "overnight" success. Because it is typical of the genesis of a play, it should be told.

Julie continues.

"From the beginning, Charlie said, 'We've got to *do* something. He and his friend Timothy Helgeson began to work together and did a lot of research. They put together materials they would like to use. They spent a lot of time thinking about it as a television play with all the other characters in it and ideally filming it in Amherst, at the house. But they were going to use the father, the mother, the sister, the brother, the sister-in-law, and all the children!

"At that point, I kept very quiet because that sort of wrung my heart. I didn't think it should be that; it would make the play something else again. The personal thing is what interested me. I wanted to use *her* words. I didn't want them diluted or covered up. I just wanted to hear *her*. That went on for about six or seven years.

"Then Timothy Helgeson met Bill Luce. Bill is a poet, and Timothy told him about this project, and so Bill was brought in to work on it.

"First he wrote a version that had a lot of people in it. And they tried to get Hallmark to do it, but couldn't. And then they wrote a version that was just a one woman play, and Charlie tried to sell that and couldn't.

"Nobody wanted to touch it on television or in the theatre either. Charlie said, somebody (I forget who) thought the idea of *me* doing Emily Dickinson was *ludicrous*."

She laughs with pleasure.

"And then, in 1974, I was in *In Praise of Love* with Rex Harrison, and Charlie was doing *God's Favorite* by Neil Simon. Charlie was sitting in Sardi's one day, being interviewed by Earl Wilson, and Don Gregory and Mike Merrick were at lunch there, too. They were in New York for their production of *Clarence Darrow* with Henry Fonda, which was about to open.

"And Charlie was talking very loudly, very exuberantly, which he always does, about this one woman play and Emily Dickinson.

"Gregory and Merrick were at another table. But they *heard* him. And they came over afterwards and said, 'We're interested in one woman plays.' He sent it over to them, and the next day they said, 'We'll do it. We'll DO IT!' And then it was *on*. And they wanted me to do it right away!"

She leans back in rapture at such a splendid story.

"Yes, I liked the play that Bill had written. There were some cute things that I tried very hard to get taken out, and most of those were, I think. You know, you live with a thing for such a long time, and it goes through a lot of changes."

The play opened on April 28, 1976, in New York, after first previewing in Seattle, Denver, Chicago, and Boston. It received tremendous reviews, was an immediate hit, ran for almost a year, and then it went on the road.

"I've done that play so many times, and I *never* get tired of doing it. Look!"

She shows me a playbill from Finland where *Belle* has recently played. She appraises the actress playing Emily, who, from her photograph, seems a trifle heavy.

"Not quite right," she murmurs. "At least to my mind. You know," she says suddenly, "I can't judge anybody except myself. I mustn't measure anybody by what I want or what's ideal to me. I just have to accept that." She continues talking about *Belle*.

"It's being done in Japan and was done in Norway. People are doing Emily all over the world!

"The material is beautiful. At the end of the play I have the feeling that I'm soaring on her wings. She's holding me up and I'm floating, sailing through the air. As Emily says, 'It feels like life is ecstasy to me. Living and sensing things.'" Her face is radiant.

You will have Emily with you until you die. She is part of you.

"*Yes!* I find that these things that hit you, hit your *heart*, are the things that you should try as an actor.

"I'm not Emily. No. The *real* Emily, her source of knowledge, her imagination, is mind boggling to me. I haven't got any of those resources. I'm not brilliant with words. I'm not clever in that way."

I ask if her parents had lived to see her as Emily. Her mother had.

"She flew to Boston to see *Belle of Amherst*, and I met her at the plane. You know, in my lifetime, *Belle* was an extraordinary thing. I wanted to involve Mother, I wanted her to see the love of the work, not what party I was going to or who I was going to see. Anyway, she'd read the reviews because it opened in Seattle and Chicago, and it had gotten *raves*.

"We were in the taxi going to the hotel and she said, 'Well, you *finally* made it. After all these years.' She sort of slapped me on the back and said, 'Good for you. Good for you.' The cab shook."

Julie leans forward, intensely.

"What had I been doing all these years?" she whispers, astonished. "I mean I had been in *hits*!" (Not to mention receiving two more Tonys—for *Forty Carats* in 1968 and for *The Last of Mrs. Lincoln* in 1972, making four.)

"That was the thing about Mother that is very moving now. It's like Emily in the play saying, When Mother became my child, affection came. When I was able finally to take care of her, then we were close. Then she would say, 'I love you.' But that was a long time coming." She is quiet, remembering.

"You know, Mother and I had many clashes. My sympathy, growing up early, was with my father. I loved them both, but I never felt that I was the kind of daughter my mother wanted.

"Mother was sort of like this woman I'm playing in *Mixed Couples*. If it looked good on the surface, that was enough for her. She was sort of a hard person. To me, she didn't have an artist's soul. I didn't care about theatre parties, who you knew, who you met. But all that appealed to mother. The glamour, the parties. Who's there? What are you going to wear? Who will do your hair? And that didn't appeal to me." She laughs. "She was always criticizing me. You know, I was kind of waifish, and she'd say, 'Oh, can't you do something with your hair? Why don't you try to look pretty, like Audrey Hepburn? And why do you have to do all those religious parts?'"

Growing up, did your parents encourage you in your plan to be an actress?

"Well, they didn't *discourage* me. Mother adored the theatre. When she was a little girl, all her paper dolls were actresses. Mother and Father used to go to the theatre all the time. They adored Fred Astaire and Fanny Brice, Gertrude Lawrence, Helen Hayes, Katharine Cornell, Ethel Barrymore. I can remember my mother imitating Ethel Barrymore in *Declassée*. 'That's all there is, there isn't any more.' Or she'd imitate Florence Reed in *The Shanghai Gesture*. 'They sewed pebbles in my feet, but I *survived*.' My mother could imitate the timbre of the voices that had been so effective to her.

"She said to me once, 'You know, *I* could have been an actress.' She held it in for years. But I knew she was sort of living vicariously through what happened to me."

Who, then, gave you the kind of emotional encouragement you needed?

"I got it from my father, sort of by osmosis. He transmitted to me, in so many ways, the knowledge that I was loved by him. Perfectly. Good and bad. That's always supported me through my life." She is whispering again. "There were others, too. Charlotte Perry. Miss Hewitt."

When you are performing, is there some part of you that's looking at yourself from the outside?

"Not when you're completely involved." Then she reconsiders. "If there's an audience there, some part of you is always checking so that you don't lose yourself completely. You see, you have to shift things; you have to be able to arrange things and send them out, here, there, everywhere. So a part of you has got to be aware of that. But usually you get very involved, so you forget yourself and the outside world.

"With the *Belle of Amherst*, there is this terrific responsibility. You can't say to the management, I don't feel well enough to do it! There is no understudy. It couldn't be, ever, half-done. I *had* to be able to go on eight times a week, one way or another. The tears had to flow, and the heart had to break. It *had* to be or else nobody was going to *listen*!

"And so there were only a few times, in the whole time I've done the play, when it was not right. When you'd say, 'I want my money back.' Because it was do or die, it was life or death. No two ways about it. I couldn't do it half way; I couldn't do it without doing it *completely*.

"It cost me a lot in energy. I had to take care of myself like a baby. My faith had to be very strong, because it wasn't *me*. I was called to do Emily. Something helped me do it. And I never lost my voice, never missed a performance, and we did it for almost a year."

When you are working to find the inner part of a character and it is not going well, do you doubt that it will ever come? And what helps you through those doubts?

"We were working on the second act yesterday. It was coming along, in a way. But then we ran through it at the end of the day, and I was out of it. I was tired and seemed to be always a beat behind everybody else (Geraldine Page, Rip Torn, and Michael Higgins). Part of me had been watching Gerry and the transformation that was taking place in her.

"I thought to myself, 'What are *you* doing? Get *with* it.' I felt empty at every moment. I came home and looked in the mirror and said, 'You see, it isn't easy. It's not just being there, not just saying the lines. You've got to fill every moment.' To do that you get involved in the physical life of the play, which is there every minute. You pick something up, you get involved with that. The whole physical process of the play has got to be worked in; when it is, you won't be without something to do.

"You realize how extraordinary the problem of acting a play is. Every moment has got to be fulfilled. It's not enough to say 'I know the lines.'

"It's only in the last few years that I don't anticipate. My idea now is to fulfill just this moment, right now, and get something that will carry you on to the next from this one. In other words, don't anticipate. Let every moment feed you into the next. That's what it is. Give and take. Listening and reacting."

Julie Harris has played everything from Shakespeare to musical comedies, farces and melodramas to tragedies. Those who have seen almost everything she's done say she's entirely believable in all the roles, no matter whom she plays. Nevertheless, something changed drastically in the way she worked in 1970 or 1971. It was while she was playing Anna Reardon, the unstable, sexually starved sister in *And Miss Reardon Drinks a Little*. Suddenly there was a new feeling of freedom that she had not known earlier.

"I had been working for almost thirty years." There is great laughter. "I learn very slowly.

"When John Geilgud and Ralph Richardson did *Home*, John Geilgud said that finally he was no longer nervous. Well, he'd been acting for maybe forty, forty-five years. It takes a *long* time. It is when the soul is free of the world and does not say, 'Am I going to be good enough? Am I going to keep up my part? Are they going to like me?' You throw *all* that *out!* You don't feel that in rehearsal!

"No, it's not all out of me now," she says with irritation. "I'm still working on it."

Do you still get nervous?

"Yes."

How do you handle that?

She looks as though she's in pain. "I want to start taking Yoga. I do a lot of relaxing exercises, breathing, and that helps somewhat." There is a long pause while she searches my face.

"I don't know how to get over that real fear. Sometimes I'll do a play—this past winter I did *On Golden Pond*. George Schaefer directed it, with my old friend Charlie Durning, whom I adore. To be on the stage with Charlie is to feel no fear, literally.

"But sometimes there is an emotional scene that's a sort of jump, like a horse you have to jump. Not so in the *Belle of Amherst*, because it was total, and I could start and sort of wend my way through it. But it's whenever the script says, 'and she cries,' and you realize you've really got to cry, right at that moment.

"You've got to find your way to do that, and sometimes my mind will say 'You're not going to be good enough to *do* that when it's really important to do it. You could do it when nobody's looking, in rehearsal when nobody cares if it's nothing and nobody has paid $10 or $20 to see it.'

"There's a small voice that says, 'It's going to be coming and you have to do it right, and you can't, can you?' So there's a division, and that's the beginning of fear."

What do you tell that small voice?

Julie Harris • 129

"You have to say, I *can* do it. And if you can't, well, you can't. It's not going to be the end of the world. You know the feeling is there; only the fear, the anxiety, is going to keep you from doing it. If your body is rigid with anxiety, you can't perform. Yoga, a sort of self-hypnosis, exercises, and relaxation are the only things that can get you over the barrier."

Do you think there's going to come a time when you've completely gotten over the fear?

"Yes I do. Definitely. Because I know it can happen when there is absolute trust between actors."

I ask her if it is possible for her to act when, in her personal life, she's been extremely upset.

"Sometimes great emotion will freeze you. About a year ago, I had gone through something very traumatic in a day, and the crisis was so extreme that I thought, 'How am I going to live through these next moments?' And I had to go on the stage.

"I did *Belle* then, like a sleepwalker, but the emotion was pretty raw. I was giving off what I felt, channeling it into the play. People came back afterward and said, 'I never saw anything like that.' And I thought, 'That's right. That was absolutely the real thing.'"

I gather from all that you've been saying that you are not completely satisfied with your work in each performance?

"NO!" She is amazed that I would ask that.

"No," she repeats. "It's *always* unpredictable. I suppose that's why it's such a challenge, because you can't say, Now *today* it's going to be fine. You can't predict it. We're human. It's not something that you can put on within certain dimensions. It's something of the flesh and something of the spirit, and it's *unpredictable!*"

Her life as an actress has not been one of unrelieved successes. In spite of five Tonys (the last for Emily), countless awards, honorary degrees, White House and royal presentations, the roles are not always hers for the asking. And though the last time she had to read for a part was for *I Am a Camera* (the producers told her to wear her sexiest dress; the playwright, John van Druten, said that after three lines of listening to her read, he never noticed what she was wearing), she has had to convince directors she was right for a role. Sometimes it didn't work.

"I wanted terribly much to do that part in *Reflections in a Golden Eye*. Originally, it was going to be done by a different director, and then the project shifted to John Huston. He wanted Margaret Leighton. I told my agent to try to get me to read for it. When she finally set it up she said, 'Huston doesn't think you're right; he doesn't really want you, but he'll look at a screen test if you do one scene.' So I did that here, a little scene, and the test was sent to him. Reluctantly he said, well, O.K. And I did the part." Alison was one of her finest screen appearances.

And she wanted the part that Liza Minelli took in *Tell Me That You Love Me, Junie Moon*. But Otto Preminger wouldn't even *see* her for it.

"He said, 'No, no, she's wrong for the part.' Well you might say I missed *that* one. [The film was not a success.] But they [the producers] seemed to have a wrong feeling about it. It was just as if the book hadn't been written, so it really could be made again.

"The girl, you know, looks more like *me*, sort of nothing. I mean I have the sort of face that, put it on and it becomes something else. It's not there to begin with. I haven't got very striking features," she says matter-of-factly.

How can you say that, I cry, dazzled by the faces she's shown me. Your face is so *alive*!

"Well, it's alive," she smiles.

Granted you don't look like Greta Garbo.

"No. I am not cosmetically beautiful. The illusion in the theatre is what is so wonderful. Remember *The Au Pair Man*? It's just a two character play. Mrs. Rogers is this extraordinary woman. Margaret Rutherford could have played the part. You see, it doesn't matter what you look like, as long as you have some kind of fascination or allure. In the theatre, what counts is character.

"But with the camera, the heroine should be beautiful. The camera requires that. And there are so many beauties—and the competition! If I were a beautiful girl, I would have another kind of worry, because you know how many beautiful women there are? They *dazzle* you. Vanessa Redgrave and Elizabeth Taylor and Samantha Eggar, one right after another. Dazzling, beautiful women!

"I once saw Vivien Leigh in Sardi's. It was toward the end of her life, and by this time I had idolized her and Olivier. And I looked into her eyes and tears sprang out of *mine*, she was so beautiful. *So* beautiful."

I think I understand what Julie Harris does. She renders space and time obsolete.

In the few brief hours we talked, a veritable population appeared in her living room. Miss Hewitt, Charles Nelson Reilly, a poor juggler, Charlotte Brontë, a man on the street whom she had met by chance as they both stood admiring photographs of movie stars, her mother, Charlie Durning, Geraldine Page, Donald Cook, Laurette Taylor, Ethel Barrymore, Ethel Waters, Emily Dickinson, Dora Carrington, George Schaefer—all flared briefly to life with her vivid portrayals. Mind you, these weren't elaborate impersonations. These were essences of what she felt was important about these people who had touched her life, sketched in gesture and voice.

Sometimes it would be a phrase about them; sometimes a line of theirs she would repeat, mimicking their voices. Sometimes it would be a description; for a couple of them, she created an entire miniscene.

Yet they all *lived* because of her. They leaped off pages of dry biography, out of scripts, out of memory and friendship, and they lived brilliantly. And that is what she brings to us on the stage—ourselves, in a much better translation.

8

THE PAINTER

Alice Neel

We thread our way into her apartment through dozens of canvases lining the hallways, two or three deep. George struggles to get his photo equipment through. Alice Neel is seated in an electric lounger chair, in the room in which she paints. An easel holds a nearly completed picture of Gus Hall, head of the Communist Party in the United States, and more canvases stand around this room.

"You're here!" she cries. "Do I know you?"

"I feel as though I know you," I tell her. "I know many of your paintings."

"That's *nice!*"

She looks me over, has me turn around. "How tall are you? You look longer waisted than you are. It's that jacket you're wearing. You have some teeth missing?" she asks. (I do.) She says she never studied anatomy but knows the structure of teeth and what they do to the face. Later, she will examine my mouth with her finger, ascertaining which teeth are where they ought to be and which are missing.

She wants to know what nationality George is, and we talk about Croatia, his father's land, and Tito.

The room, besides being filled with canvases, is stacked high with magazines, mail, art catalogs. So is the fireplace. Splendid pieces of sculpture stand around—a poised, fierce cat, in bronze; a bust of Alice Neel's mother; a figure in which the arm is separate from the torso. All of the sculptures are alive, demanding, and *hers*.

"I did all of them in '54. Then I had arthritis, and the doctor said, 'You can't do sculpture, you'll ruin yourself.' So I gave it up. Isn't it a shame? Believe me, I could do some great sculpture, because I had other ideas, too.

"If you see the devil, you offer him my soul in exchange for twenty more years. Will you?"

I tell her I see the devil *frequently*.

"Well, you tell him that my soul may be rather motheaten and damaged, but it still has some sparks in it and that you'll give it to him to take to hell with him if he'll give me twenty more years of life."

The phone rings. She motions me to answer, and I hand her the receiver. It's the gallery in Detroit where she is having a show the following week, in conjunction with a slide lecture she's giving at Wayne State University. Afterwards, she's to fly to Baltimore for another show and slide lecture. She says I must really get up to Long Island to see a third show of hers and it's a pity that I missed the one in Boston that just closed. But there's a small show going on in New York right now that I might make.

She unzips her dress. "Come here and feel my pacemaker. I just had it put in and it's wonderful. Tomorrow I can talk with you in the morning, but in the afternoon I have to go into the hospital for an electrocardiogram. Next year, guess what? I can do it on the telephone! Just put the receiver up to my pacemaker, and they'll take the electrocardiogram from that."

The phone rings again. I answer it and hand her the receiver. This time, it's the foundry about casting one of her sculptures.

She hangs up and the phone rings again. Her daughter-in-law, Nancy Neel, takes it this time. It's a photographer who's doing a book about bathtubs with naked people in them and wants her to pose.

"He only wants me because I painted that nude self-portrait, and I don't want to be lionized as semipornographic. Did you see it in *Newsweek*? But that painting is not how I look. I look *sweet* in it, don't I? A dumb little Anglo-Saxon face."

Like a fox, says George.

"Yes, dumb like a fox, that's right." She grins.

"Isn't it a miracle I've lived this long?" she asks happily.

Alice Neel is eighty-one. She just celebrated her birthday. Dozens of guests attended a party given for her by millionaire Stewart Mott, whom she has painted.

"I couldn't eat my cake. I'm diabetic, too."

She also has cataracts and arthritis, but her face is almost free of wrinkles, her green eyes glitter with life, her cheeks are pink and she could pass for a woman in her sixties.

I think it *is* a miracle—not that she's lived to be eighty-one, but that she is still working, still producing, still doing the paintings that *she* wants to do, after sixty years. The paintings have literally nothing to do with trends in art. Never have had. That's why, perhaps, she has never made the cover of *Art News*, an affront that still hurts. It wasn't until 1972 that the Whitney Museum in New York even hung one of her works, and not until 1974 did she receive the belated but deserved recognition for her work in a Whitney retrospective. Fifty-eight of her paintings, covering a lifetime, were finally brought together in one of the most prestigious museums of modern art in the United States. She has mixed feelings about the Whitney. About her show there, she says, "You know, for the first time in my life, I thought I had a right to paint. Because I was in the Whitney." But later on in our conversation she berates the Whitney for showing an artist like Andy Warhol:

"Nine years from Brillo boxes to a Whitney show," she moans.

Last year, Alice Neel was cited as one of the five best living women painters, an award presented by President Jimmy Carter in the Oval Office.

So now the television crews come, from here and abroad; now the interview requests pour in; and now the one person shows all over the country—shows she needed decades ago.

Why was Alice Neel virtually ignored during the first two-thirds of her life? For one thing, Alice Neel was painting pictures of people when abstract artists were ruling the art world.

For another thing, there were the paintings themselves. It is important to understand that her paintings of people are not portraits. "A portrait is, as Whistler said, 'when there is something wrong with the nose.' 'Portraits' hang in the Harvard Club and other stuffy surroundings," she says, "and they are usually commissioned."

Says Alice, "I avoided commissions. I never painted for money, although I'd sell paintings because I needed money to live. But you know what it was? Up until 1959, it was hard for anybody to accept my paintings. They said I was too brutal."

You see, Alice Neel's paintings strip her subjects of the facade they ordinarily present to the world. Under her brush, human beings are revealed in all of their pain, sorrow, anger, malcontent, and fear.

Naked, figuratively and otherwise, they stare out of her canvases in resignation. Between them and us there are no secrets. We know these people; we've seen their expressions before; in them we recognize ourselves.

Though her paintings compel us to confront the human condition, bad as it is, she doesn't leave us there, hanging. A vulnerable hand, a fragile foot, a worried eyebrow, a toe scrunched up nervously, an agitated thumb acknowledge our human frailties, our weaknesses.

I can think of only three or four paintings that are entirely what she calls brutal, but there are many that are hard to take.

She also paints life around her, though not as frequently as she used to. A satirical painting done immediately after her return from her first trip to Europe in 1965 is entitled "The Great Society." In it, life's elderly and downtrodden sit in mute despair in a New York cafeteria. During the Depression, Alice painted a bored and impassive committee investigating poverty; another, entitled "Nazis Murder Jews," was of a torchlight parade in 1937, a parade at which Alice was arrested. She has painted courtrooms; a suicide ward in a hospital; a "Well Baby Clinic" that is a travesty on the words. "Futility of Effort," which she feels is her best work, is a painting of a dead infant that had hung itself in the slats of a crib.

In the 1930's, she painted nudes when people were just getting used to the nudes of Renoir. Of "Ethel Ashton," a stunningly composed painting showing a corpulent, placid woman, Alice says, "That's an amazing painting, a very revolutionary painting, for 1930. Nobody was doing nudes like that."

In 1933 she even painted a male nude, "Joe Gould," who sported a triple set of genitalia. Her "Degenerate Madonna" was so objectionable to the Catholic churches in the area that it had to be withdrawn from a sidewalk show in

Washington Square in 1932. She delights in adding that in 1976, she was commissioned by Rome to paint Archbishop Jean Jadot, who is now a cardinal.

In 1940 she painted Audrey McMahon, head of the WPA Art Project in New York, as a witch. Alice did not like Audrey. "Nobody liked Audrey," she cries. "She was the one who gave out the pink slips that fired you!"

The McMahon painting hangs in her apartment, brimming over with baleful malevolence. But it won't for long. Alice is going to donate it to the National Gallery of Art in Washington, D.C., which has requested it as part of its permanent exhibit.

"Don't you think it would be more important in the National Gallery than hanging here?"

Couldn't they buy it? I ask.

"Well, they should, but I can't tell *them*. I have too many manners!"

To Alice Neel, human beings are the vital record of history: To paint them is to paint history, to capture the *zeitgeist*.

"I believe in the historical importance of art and that more is communicated about our era and its effect on people by a revealing portrait than in any other way," she wrote in the *New York Times* in 1976.

And earlier, in her doctoral address at her alma mater, Moore College of Art, Alice Neel explained: "I decided to paint a human comedy, such as Balzac had done in literature.... . I painted the neurotic, the mad and the miserable. Also I painted the others, including some squares ... Like Chichikov (in Gogol's *Dead Souls*), I am a collector of souls. Now, some of my subjects are beginning to die and they have an historic nostalgia. Everyone seems better and more important when they are dead. If I could, I would make the world happy. The wretched faces in the subway, sad and full of troubles worry me."

She points out another reason her work was not recognized earlier.

"I was a woman. That was partly it. Women are second class citizens, and they still are," she cries. "Did you read *A Room of One's Own*, by Virginia Woolf?"

No.

"Then you know nothing about feminism! Why are you so stupid? That was written in 1929. Just go and get that book, at the library, if necessary. It is *wonderful*. It shows the subtle and actual discrimination against women."

She sighs. "But then women can't do everything. I hate to see women give up being mothers. It's just that they're trying so hard to get recognition. Part of it is good, but the part that's bad is when they blame the whole thing on men and when they resent men so. The men did have the advantage, but you can't throw them out of life, you know."

Abruptly, she recalls some of the critics that drove her crazy with stupid remarks. "One said, 'The trouble with you is you're too *literary*!' Another said, 'You're just using regular paint and easels.' (Those were the days of Sigueiros, with housepaint on the walls.) Somebody else said, 'You're just painting *one* person!' Everything they said was stupid. It didn't faze me; I didn't change."

Then she thinks more about her career and why it took so long for her work to be recognized.

Being a woman was some of it, she finally decides, but mostly it was what she painted and how. In short, Alice Neel was an expressionist painter in an abstract world. "I believe that objective reality exists, but then I take certain liberties. And *that* is expressionism!

"I'm not against abstraction, by the way," she says. "I think every good picture has a large element of abstraction, although they'd die to hear me say that. But guess what? I don't think abstraction exists. I'll tell you why. I don't think the human brain is capable of inventing a shape. You know what abstractionists do? They mix together all these things, distort shapes, and put together things that have no relation, but they don't invent. They *think*, and there is a certain amount of invention in that, *but a basic shape is not invented*. It is *seen* first. And guess who agrees with this? Picasso. But I had this conviction for years, that the human brain, just from a perceptual level, was not capable of really inventing a shape."

That's about as far as Alice Neel will go analyzing her work and what it is not. She shuns rules, hates theories, and does not approach art intellectually. A lot of my questions went out the window when I realized this, but as they did, a lot of fresh air came in.

For example, when I ask if there is a certain moment when she knows she wants to do a painting, she answers impatiently,

"Oh what difference does it make? I don't know the exact moment in anything. I never analyzed myself to that extent. But I formed the habit of translating life into art early."

As a child in Colwyn, Pennsylvania, she remembers carefully drawing studies of violets and Roses of Sharon. Her father was a railroad clerk for the Pennsylvania Railroad. *His* father had been a Civil War veteran, and there were several opera singers in the family. Her mother was descended from one of the signers of the Declaration of Independence. Alice was the third of four children, two brothers and a sister.

"My mother would say to me, 'I don't know what you expect to do in the world, Alice. You're only a girl!'"

How did that make you feel? I ask.

"Ambitious," she grins.

George is photographing her while we talk. She has been looking agreeably pleasant for him.

"Can I be very serious once?" she asks plaintively. "Can I be like I really am? You know, I used to have these aunts that would come and see me, and I would pinch my cheeks so they'd be pink. And I used to *smile*. But I wasn't a bit like that, you know. I wasn't a sweet, smiley little thing."

What were you like as a little girl?

"I was an unknown quantity. That's what my mother used to say."

But she always knew she was going to be an artist.

"When I was in high school, I loved botany class. We had a bean that sprouted, and I made beautiful drawings of the bean and the sprouting. They looked like Ellsworth Kelly drawings. And guess what? I would draw profiles of people, but I didn't have the courage to do them in the center of the paper. I did them so that the back of the head was right on the edge of the sheet. I was absolutely terrified of that whole sheet of paper!"

In contrast, she recalls beginning the large painting of Moses and Raphael Soyer, brothers who were known for their paintings of social realism in the 1930s. The canvas was a large one, 60 by 46 inches, and as she began drawing swiftly and surely on the large expanse, Moses remarked that she was terribly brave to attack that huge space. That memory pleases her. If there is one thing that has happened in her life of painting, Alice Neel has lost her terror of blank spaces.

I ask her if she ever doubts her work.

"You doubt it all the time. *SURE*. But you want to know something interesting? I read it recently. Somebody said all work is produced in the hullabaloo that life is. You know it *is* a hullabaloo." She stares intently at me to be sure I agree.

"Do you have children?" she asks.

Yes.

"How many?"

Two.

"Then you know."

Alice Neel has two sons: Richard, who is a lawyer in New York, and Hartley, who is a radiologist in Vermont.

"You know," she says softly, "I never could have had a career in art without those children."

I tell her I'm surprised to hear that.

"You know why? Because I had to have some emotional involvement. The father of the youngest child was a brilliant fellow but absolutely crazy, always running around the country. I used to be glad he was away because he was so difficult to live with. He was violent. But he was a genius. He's the man that did that wonderful photograph of me. I don't give his name. I just call him my Russian lover. He always resented the other boy who wasn't his son. It was difficult. He was a bad stepfather. So I was glad when he went away."

I ask how she managed to make a living when her sons were small; when her mates were not exactly helpful with the rent.

She looks at me hard, with those bright eyes boring.

"You know what I told somebody that asked me that at the Metropolitan Museum? 'I used to go pick dollars off the trees.' That's what I told him."

But you kept right on painting then. How did you manage? I persist.

"That's right. But it's for me to know and you to find out. Isn't that mean?"

You don't want to talk about it then.

"No. I won't go into the finances. It's too difficult. It was utterly painful." We look at one another intently.

"Oh, it was horrible. I had to be a very clever person. I had my children in a private school. You know what I did at that private school?"

Then she changes the subject.

"You know what? To be an artist you have to have two things—the will of the devil and you have to love art. Those things are absolutely contradictory. To love art is the absorption of pleasure; to have the will of the devil is a thing you have to impose on yourself."

I, too, change the subject.

Are you completely satisfied with your work when you've finished with it?

"NO, NO," she almost shouts. "I am much *wilder* than my work! My work is more conservative than I am and that comes from the world. The world cuts you down. When you say how do you take care of all those things, there's always frightful bills, there's Medicare, there's the rent, there's gas and light; and they all have such strict laws, God help you if you miss them. There's everything that you *have* to do.

"When my children were young, I wouldn't even read *Art News*, because art had such a powerful fascination for me and I wasn't in the running. Because even though I painted good pictures, I didn't show them anywhere very much."

Later on, the next day, we are talking once again about the children, and she says softly,

"About how I earned my living in those years. I guess the reason I didn't want to talk about it was, it was distasteful to me.

"I used to give classes sometimes. There are a lot of women that study art, at menopause age. I had them come to the house. There is a menopausal artist, you know. Well, their children are grown. It's a mean thing to say, really. I shouldn't say it, because it's perfectly all right to study art at any age, but they're in the late forties, fifties. And they're *nice*. But even though fifty people study art, you maybe only get one artist out of it." She is strangely subdued, for Alice.

It isn't a bad thing to give classes, I tell her. Do you mind if I say that you held classes in order to live?

"No. I don't mind at all."

The classes were in the 1940s.

Earlier, Alice Neel worked for the WPA Public Works Project in New York in 1933. And in 1935 she joined the WPA Easel Project, for which she was required to turn out a painting every six weeks.

"That was nothing for me. I could do a painting for them in two days." She was paid $26.88 a week for her work. I ask her what happened to all those paintings.

"Don't you know about that scandal? All of those paintings of the WPA Art Project were sold by the government as oiled canvases to wrap pipe in!"

Both of us scream in pain.

I ask how she felt, working for the government.

"When I was on the WPA, I was a much better artist than any of them, because I was already developed. I had already done "Futility of Effort," a very sophisticated picture. It is simple, and it has a beautiful design.

"So in the beginning, I felt superior. But then, because of the days and that same old *zeitgeist*, I began to think that anybody that really loved art should be able to get on the WPA, because they could learn there and it would keep them from starving. It's not nice to see people dying of starvation!" She glares at me.

I ask, from the benefit of hindsight, how the WPA seems to her now.

"Listen, dear, there was no choice. It was *those days*. We choose, to a certain extent, but we don't choose the times. The WPA was a great thing. But so was the theatre project. All of them were. It not only kept those people from starving, but it was *culture*."

We talk about learning art.

"I believe in learning to draw. Drawing is the discipline of art. You learn to draw two ways. You think about it all the time, you're always working at it—that's one way. And you are taught drawing if you go to art school, but not everybody learns!

"I went to a conventional art school. I went to the Philadelphia School of Design for Women (now Moore College of Art) from 1921 to 1925. I had occasional classes before, but not really art school. We drew first from plaster casts, and I don't think that's a bad beginning. The school had the most magnificent collection of Italian masterpieces—"Moses," which I drew, and the Elgin marbles. A much better collection than even the Victoria and Albert Museum in England.

"And I was good at drawing and won all the prizes. But what I also had was a fantastic memory. I trained it. I *made* myself paint from memory something I saw every day.

"I'll tell you an interesting thing about memory. It stands you in good stead even if you paint someone from life. Do you know that when John Singer Sargent taught art in London, he made the model sit in one room and the students draw in another room? They would have to memorize while they went into the other room.

"I did it another way. I trained myself. Every day I'd draw something from memory, and some of my pictures, quite a few of the well-known ones, are from memory. I had so trained myself that I could remember for twelve hours. You have to look at *everything*, the relation of the arm to the hand, for instance, because you don't do just one portion, you do the entire figure."

She painted her father in his coffin the day after his funeral, without sketching it or memorizing it either. "That made such an impact on me. I knew I'd never see him again."

Once, years later, she and her sons went for a walk in the park. They were living in Spanish Harlem at the time.

"I saw this Spanish woman with a pink velvet hat, and as I told you, I had trained myself to remember things. So when the boys took a nap that afternoon, I painted a masterpiece!

"And it was even better because no one was posing, so I could be freer. It was one of the best pictures I ever painted."

Why does she think so?

"The expressionist quality. The fact that it's very unconventional in form."

Nancy Neel, Alice's daughter-in-law, brings out a slide of the painting. A proud woman gazes out at you. On her face is the certain knowledge that this is all of life. On her head, however, is the glorious pink velvet hat to lend glory, however momentary, to that life.

"Isn't that gorgeous?" she says. "Look at the technique of the face. It's just as expressionist as any of them. I *love* that. I think, maybe, my mother would say to me, 'Alice, that picture is just grand.'"

Though there were many street scenes and cityscapes in her work, Alice Neel always worked at home.

"When I did the street scenes, I'd go out and make a sketch and write in the colors. As I told you, I have this great memory, I could then paint it at home. I couldn't paint in the streets, ever, because people gather around and that made me nervous. For me, painting is one hundred percent concentration."

Tell me, Alice Neel, when you see a painting that really knocks you out, how do you feel inside?

"It doesn't knock me out. It *stimulates* me!"

I press for details. How do you feel?

There is a great burst of laughter.

"How do I feel? Well, I don't know if I feel quite as good as after an orgasm, but *almost* as good! Is that too indecent? I'm not sure which is better. I think maybe the orgasm is better because it's more direct. But I do think that you get off the ground. You get out of yourself. It's a *terrific* connection with life," she cries.

Picasso is one of those painters who stimulates her.

"Look, he stimulates the *whole world*! Picasso not only was a great painter, but he reviewed *all* painting. You see, he could borrow without being a plagiarist like————, up at the Academy of Arts and Letters."

In an article, Alice Neel said about Picasso, "Picasso *is* the twentieth century." She brings out a catalog from the recent Picasso retrospective at the Museum of Modern Art.

"I went four times to that show because the Museum of Modern Art has something of mine. I went in a wheelchair, and I took someone along to push it. I would even get in about a half-hour before it opened. Picasso's father was his art teacher, taught him painstakingly to do pigeon's legs. And one day when Picasso did a whole pigeon, his father handed him his palette, knowing that Picasso was better than he. Yes, I believe in learning to draw. When you want to take the world apart like Picasso does, he knows everything so perfectly that he can take any kind of liberty with it. He knows it *all*, and he chooses.

"You know what I said in that article? That Picasso even involves the composition of the person with the furniture and other things in the room. That they *all* participate in it."

She finds an early painting of Picasso's in the catalog and calculates how old he was when he painted it. "Seventeen or eighteen," she announces. "When Picasso was twelve, he knew all the secrets of conventional art. Look at it," she cries. "It's expert. Now, many an artist, struggling for years—until he's about forty—will finally paint like this, but he'll paint like this for the rest of his life!

"Picasso, of course, deserves credit for *working*. You know what he said? He *didn't* say I was a born genius. Know what he said? 'I was born with an obsession for hard work.' Even as an old, old man in his eighties, he did those very sensual drawings."

She settles back and closes her eyes. I begin to ask another question.

"Wait a minute. Wait a minute!" She holds up her hand. "I have to take a rest. Too much electricity, too much on the wire." She pats the pacemaker.

Later, she apologizes. "I am so avid for everything and so interested, I use myself up. I don't have as much strength as I used to have." She looks at me and grins. "You know, I am eighty-one, so I can just take so much. The CAT scanner said I was only fifty in my brain. That's great, but still my brain is attached to all this other me. I may look young, but I walk like I'm ninety."

She gestures at her body, which is plump, but which clearly doesn't respond to her directions the way it used to, and she doesn't like it.

Suddenly she asks, what do you think of Gus Hall?

Gus Hall is the Communist leader who is currently sitting for Alice. His painting is nearly finished except for the hand. This hell raiser, this man of picket lines and confrontation, is curiously benign in Alice's portrait.

"See, he has no bureaucracy in his nature," she points out.

How did painting him come about?

"He saw a film made about me [*The Originals*], and he loved it. So I realized he was a very openminded guy, because your ordinary stuffy Communist wouldn't like it. In the film they asked me about the Communist Party, and I said, 'Oh, I joined several times.'" She laughs. "And Gus Hall said that was wonderful. But a real bureaucratic Communist would criticize me for that, say I was frivolous or something.

"So then he heard they wanted to give me a show in Russia, but that the Embassy in Washington was slow about it. So I proposed to his secretary that he come over and pose for me. She said, 'Oh, he'd *love* to.' He came over three times, one after the other. And the next one very soon, because I don't like the work to get cold."

She casts a critical eye at the painting.

"That picture can stand a well-done hand because the other things are well-done too: It won't throw it out of balance."

Does Gus Hall like it?

"He thinks it's wonderful. He said it even looks like his father."

What if the subject doesn't like it?

"When they are stupid, I don't care. They suffer a little. But guess what?" She tells me about an artist who posed for her, but did not really believe in Alice's kind of art. "I had given her a crazy expression, like a sailor on shore leave. When I had finished, she said, 'Well, it's not one of your good figure pieces.' But when her confreres came here, they *loved* it. And they bought it!" she crows. "They had just built a new museum to house the Roy Lichtensteins and the Klaes Oldenburgs. So when she went in there, the first thing she saw was her own portrait. And wait until I show you what advertising does. She now *loves* it. Why? Because somebody else likes it. AMAZING! They have eaten up my soul," she cries with joy and pain.

Cindy Nemser, art editor and writer, who wrote the introduction for the Georgia Museum of Art show catalog, *Alice Neel*, was painted, along with her husband Chuck Nemser, by Alice. They were both in the nude.

Nemser describes first how both she and her husband progressed from complete opposition to a nude portrait to final resignation and acceptance of Alice Neel's plan.

In the painting, "we sat close together, holding hands in an attitude of mutual support. My body concealed Chuck's sexual parts while his hand rested on my waist in a gesture of affectionate protectiveness. In this double portrait, Alice had psyched us out as individuals and had also arrived at the essence of our relationship."

Nemser also reports that when Alice painted the torsos and hands, she talked or made comments, but when she began painting the faces she became silent, transfixed, totally oblivious to anything but the painting.

In an article for the *New York Times* in 1976, Alice wrote about painting from her own point of view.

I am never arbitrary. Before painting, I talk to my sitters and they unconsciously assume their most typical pose, which in a way involves all their character and social standing, what the world has done to them and their retaliation. What I feel, what I think and my involvement with the sitter all comes out in the painting. I like it to look spontaneous, not labored.

I enjoy dividing that white, unsullied canvas according to the composition that best interprets the person. Usually, I place everything when I start by drawing on the canvas in blue or black paint, directly from the model. . . .

I do not think consciously of technique; I do not believe one should concentrate on technique. I feel the art in my work is the way I do it, an ongoing thing that happens when I work.

"Do you know what I do?" Alice asks. "I sometimes draw the whole thing, and sometimes I paint it as I go along. But usually I do both together.

"But I don't think of any theory, I don't think of any style or anything else when I'm painting. The reason is the subconscious participates in art. Sometimes your conscious mind ruins your art, and your subconscious saves it. If you do something and don't even know why, perhaps that's the best thing you do. So I just blot out everything from my mind and concentrate."

She can only work a couple of hours at a time.

"Painting is hard work. It isn't fun. In two hours you're exhausted because you've used all your faculties."

Well, there is a "fun" part, she admits. It's after the session, sitting down and just looking at the painting. That she enjoys.

I ask her if it is difficult while the painting is in progress to keep in mind the original concept of it.

"That's where a good memory comes in. Some people are so mercurial that one has to remember the original concept. One three-quarter length portrait of Walter Gutman I painted in my head two years before I actually did it."

She has called her subjects "victims." I ask her if she really thinks of them that way.

"I *say* that. You know why? Because that's the way they think. No, I don't think they're victims, but it just makes for more interesting English than to say models."

She'll frequently get up in the middle of the night and "fix something" on a painting that isn't right. But then, "at a certain point, I know it's finished because I'm bored with it."

There is one exception, an extremely large painting, "Nancy and the Rubber Plant," painted in 1975. "That one I worked on for over a period of a month. I even had to get up on a stepladder to do the top of it. But I never lost interest in it, and I don't know why. I can't explain it."

She looks at me and shakes her head.

Does your work age well for you? Is it satisfying to look back at what you've done?

"Look. The only reason you keep painting is that you always think you can do better."

Then you get discouraged with your work?

"Suicidal!" she shouts.

Can you work, then, if you are upset or angry?

"I prefer not to be upset. You know what I am? I'm a trained neurotic. They're the best people."

What do you mean by that?

"I had a frightful breakdown, and you don't go through that without learning a lot of self-control. Even if you get into a sanitarium, the person that gets you out is yourself. You get yourself in, and you get yourself out. Now if you have such terrible things happen that you really go under, it may be hard for you to cure yourself. But *nobody else can!* You have to come around to the opinion that you don't want to be like that and fight it. It took a whole year out of my life."

That was in 1931—a terrible time for Alice Neel. She had lost her infant daughter to diptheria. Her Cuban husband, Carlos Enríquez, had left her and taken their other daughter with him to Cuba. Alice had a nervous breakdown.

"One of my lives had collapsed, and I couldn't take it. I had Freud's classic sinking spells. That is, you just die, and you know you're dying. It happens every day, and you get weaker and weaker. Didn't you read about my suicide attempt?"

Yes, I tell her I knew about it, but I hadn't planned to ask her about it or the time she spent in a Philadelphia hospital suicide ward (which she later painted). What I do want to ask is how she managed to keep painting in the midst of all that heartache and despair? Because there was not only the loss of her daughters and the break-up of her marriage. There was more pain to come.

"Art, art, art!" she cries. "I painted masterpieces!"

She had met a merchant seaman, Kenneth Doolittle. They lived together for a while in Greenwich Village, until Doolittle, in a jealous rage, slashed and burned sixty of her paintings and three hundred drawings and watercolors. It was a loss she would never get over.

"All I will tell you about that is that it was frightful. *Frightful*. I never recovered. Those losses were irrevocable. They were just *gone*. The paintings were cut and some of them burnt. The watercolors were just burnt up in a fireplace."

Few watercolors of that period survive. One of them, ironically, is of Doolittle, who had vandalized her work. It is a study of a cocky, carefree fellow, brimming over with virility and life. It is one of her best works and was recently purchased by the Hirshhorn Museum for its permanent collection.

The destruction of her work happened in 1933. Earlier that year Alice had painted the outrageous nude of Joe Gould and had dated it because she knew it would not be shown for years. The first time, in fact, was in the late 1960's.

These, now, were the WPA years, and at least she was working regularly. In 1938, she moved to Spanish Harlem with Jose Santiago. They had a son, Richard Neel, born in 1939.

"I could have a show of only paintings I did in Harlem. But the world is so snobbish and prejudiced that they won't do that. So I just, now and then, include a painting from Spanish Harlem."

Her first one person show in New York (there had been one in Cuba in 1926), was in 1938 at the Contemporary Arts Gallery.

She once said, "Nothing could be more important than that one's work be shown," and we talk about that now. "I had an audience, I had intellectuals and writers, but I didn't have the real audience. You know the best thing about a show? *You're out there*. And it's good even when it's a mixed show because you're out there with other people. You can see yourself more objectively."

In that first show at Contemporary Arts there were sixteen paintings of "people, houses, and landscapes," but it was the people that stood out and about which *Art News* commented: "Her portraits are characters made real and familiar."

There was another show that year: She was shown with seven other artists. And in 1944 she had a one person show at Rose Fried's first gallery, The Pinacotheca. But when Rose Fried supported abstract expressionism, Alice Neel left the gallery in disgust. There was not another one person show until 1950, but it was during the 1940s that Alice Neel was painting some of her best work— "Tuberculosis in Harlem," a classic study of a Puerto Rican boy, resigned in his suffering and imminent death ("I did that one for *me*, not the WPA"); an unsentimental but loving portrait of her mad Russian lover; the moving portrait of her dead father in his coffin; paintings of her mother and of her children; some powerful landscapes.

She talks about being a mother and a painter simultaneously.

"I painted all through my life. When I give lectures to young people, I tell them, If you get married and you decide to have a child, don't give up painting! For one thing, you never go back to it. For another thing, you miss all the reactions of this new situation. So you just don't give it up, that's all. Know what you really do? You domesticate it. You bring it home with you.

"Another thing, the less attention you get, there has to be some emotional nourishment. If I hadn't had these children, I never would have been able to paint, though they also made it more difficult. But I could never have shut myself up in a studio and just worked. I don't have that kind of brain. It has to be connected with life in some way.

"The more experiences you can have, the more you will develop, provided you don't go too far, because then you will die of it."

There were not a lot of paintings in the 1950s. I ask her why. Her sons were teenagers then, she explains, and she was busy with them as they grew up. But in the 1960s, Richard got married, and Hartley went off to college, and then there was more time to paint.

In 1960, Alice painted two portraits of the poet Frank O'Hara. One is a profile of a handsome, hawk-nosed, slightly arrogant looking man. The other is a frontal portrait that has the look of death about it. In it, O'Hara's teeth resemble tombstones; his skin is stretched tautly over bone. Withered flowers in the background contribute to the chilling specter of death in life that haunts the portrait.

Both paintings were hung in a show at the American Contemporary Arts Gallery in 1960, and Alice remembers that time as probably the beginning of national recognition for her work.

"I had always gotten good reviews. And I was known among all the *artists*. But when I showed this Frank O'Hara in two versions, for the first time they gave me a reproduction in *Art News*. They were crazy about it. They said there were other people showing, but they said that my stuff was so much better than anybody else's. And there was the interesting idea of doing the same person twice; different sides of him."

Stewart Mott, the well-to-do son of the board chairman of General Motors, became a school friend of Hartley's and then of Alice's. He occasionally squired her around town. Her 1961 painting of him is of a young man, slightly spoiled, but his good nature and his humor come through.

Why do we like that portrait, Alice? She does and so do I.

"It's very *living*. And it shows a person with all the advantages, don't you know?"

I know.

For that painting, she won the Longview Foundation Prize, and the painting was given to Dillard University. And slowly, it began. The recognition that had eluded her for so many years, now began to happen. In 1962, she appeared in a prestigious figure show at the Kornblee Gallery, which was shown in conjunction with another figure show at the Museum of Modern Art. Something was happening in the art world, obviously. Abstract art was slowly beginning to lose its throttle hold. Alice Neel's expressionist paintings were no longer being ignored. Her one person shows mushroomed. In the 1960s there were six of them, three at the Graham Gallery in New York City, which has represented her since 1963.

(In the 1970s, there were twenty-two one person shows. In the 1980s, so far, there has been eight.)

Now all the figures of the art world came to her studio apartment on 107th Street, cheerfully willing to be subjected to Alice Neel's scrutiny and soul scouring—critics and artists and museum directors; transvestites and poets; art dealers; black nationalists; children; married couples. And always there were new portraits of the family: Nancy, pregnant. Nancy with her newborn baby, Olivia. Nancy with the twins; Olivia in all stages of growing up. Richard and Hartley as students, and then established in their professions.

She painted sculptor Duane Hanson: "That portrait has a certain profundity."

She painted the curator of Modern Art at the Metropolitan Museum, Henry Geldzahler, in 1967: "It's powerful. It's an interesting pose." She laughs, remembering how when she got around to painting the shirt, "Henry said, 'I'll just leave the shirt here for you.' 'No, Henry,' she pointed out. "'You have to be *in* it.'"

She painted the aging artists Raphael and Moses Soyer, and the painting hung in the Whitney Museum for a month when Moses Soyer died. She painted fellow painter Isabel Bishop, composer Virgil Thomson, play producer Joseph Papp, and critics—John Gruen with his wife and daughter, Hubert Crehan, Charlotte Willard, dealer Ellie Poindexter, and dozens of others.

I've noticed that her attitude toward critics and museum people is ambivalent. She needs them, but she doesn't respect them much, and that often shows in her paintings. I say I think she doesn't care much about the critics. Her eyes blaze.

"You *have* to care about critics. They can *ruin* you," she shouts. "If they say you're good, everybody rushes to the gallery to buy. If they say you're bad, the opposite happens. Everybody listens to critics!

"But you have to live a life. If you sell paintings, you're better off than if you don't sell them."

She asks me if I know a certain person working in a museum.

No, I don't know *any* museum people, I tell her.

"You're better off," she crows.

And *galleries!*

"I will tell you something. Many people in charge of galleries don't know good from bad. And everybody changes their job! Just when you get used to an art director, they move somewhere else, and the new one doesn't know you. Just like they have people review me that never heard of me before, so it's like starting all over again!"

Do you need outside eyes to look at your work to tell you it is good?

"Yes, you *do*. You need reassurance. Of *course*. If I would go somewhere and they didn't like my work, I wouldn't get over it for six months. In 1959 I painted a wonderful portrait of Baron Eric von Eckerstrom. But I never could tell anybody because I was ashamed, portraits were considered so low then. Now look at Andy making a million. Oh they're all goddam business people," she cries.

What about the failures, the times your paintings, your work, didn't live up to your expectations?

"I don't dwell on the failures at all, except you learn from everything. I just have the canvas scraped. I don't fuss with things endlessly."

And when your paintings leave you, how do you feel?

"*Awful*. Horrible. You have to sell them, you know, but I hate to see them leave. For one thing, every painting comes out of the painting before it. You see, I never copy myself. After you finish a painting, what you see wrong with it afterwards influences your next painting. Sometimes. Not always."

What do you tell young painters who are having trouble, who get discouraged and want to give it all up?

"You see you have more trouble when you're young. You really have a hell of a time. But I tell them I can't answer that. They have to find their own road. They have to have the steam to want to do it enough to stick to it. If they don't, it's not my province at all. I just advise them not to try to go to SoHo. They're all dying to get there, but it's even more confusing there. I say that's not what you should be thinking about. It's better if you just stay where it's easier for you to be and work. And try to find out what it is you are really interested in because you don't know, always. But it's their problem. *They* have to decide whether to keep going or give it up. You can't take the responsibility of their lives, you know."

Did you ever want to give it all up?

She looks at me hard.

"What for? You have a sentence, you have to live it out."

In 1976, Alice Neel received still another honor. She—and coincidentally, Gwendolyn Brooks—were elected to the American Academy of Arts and Letters, a prestigious organization that elects its members on the basis of artistic, literary, or musical achievement and limits membership to fifty.

"I liked it," she says of the honor, "but you know what I told them? Better late than *never*."

Honors, awards, one person shows ("I've never had so many"); people coming to make films, to write books and articles about her, more money than she ever dreamed she'd get for a portrait (seven or eight years ago it was $3,000; today it is $20,000)—is all this attention and recognition giving her more freedom to paint, or is it harder?

"If you keep it under control, it's better. You can't get wildly excited about it. You have to keep your own self."

You'll never give that up, I comment.

"Well, why?" she demands. "If I have a stroke, I will. I won't mean to. There is no such word as never in the human language. Everything is for a time."

Do you think about that a lot?

"Well, I think about it more than you do, because I'm closer to the end!"

Are you afraid of the end?

"Well, I think everybody is. It's strange, too, how we've solved everything but not *that*.

"Maybe we'll get destroyed. Maybe we'll get bombed right out of the world. I don't want that. I think it's stupid. Ignorance is the *worst* thing," she cries. "Who was it that thought there was no evil, only ignorance? Or was it there is no sin, only error?"

I don't know, I say.

"I don't know either."

We have been talking for two days, talk that has excited each of us so that we haven't been able to sleep at night. We have talked about art and life, men and children, and above all, her work. We are talked out, and Alice must go to the hospital for her electrocardiogram.

We shake hands: Hers are strong and smooth and no veins show.

As George and I leave, she calls after us,

"Goodbye children. I wish more went into art and music and less to the Pentagon. Art is a positive thing, and it is a good thing."

And just before we close the door, we hear,

"If I had twenty more years of working, I know I would be a great sculptor!"

THE COMPOSER

Mary Lou Williams

At the age of three, sitting on her mother's knee, Mary Elfrieda Winn perfectly duplicated a tune her mother had just played on the organ, her tiny fingers easily finding the right keys. Her mother was so astonished, she dropped the child and ran to get a neighbor to listen.

Mary Elfrieda is now Mary Lou Williams, and she is seventy-one. Music has lifted her from her mother's lap and taken her all over the world, and vice versa. Her jazz, her music has been played by the brightest lights in an already blazing world of sound—Benny Goodman, Duke Ellington, Count Basie, the Dorsey brothers, Jimmie Lunceford, Charlie Parker, Dizzy Gillespie, Louis Armstrong.

It has been performed by the New York Philharmonic in Carnegie Hall; at the White House; at countless jazz festivals all over the world. Her jazz Mass has been lifted up in New York's St. Patrick's Cathedral and in a dozen lesser known houses of God; it has inspired new dances by choreographers Alvin Ailey and Katherine Dunham.

There isn't a jazz musician alive that doesn't owe Mary Lou Williams.

Out of all that was new in her lifetime—spirituals, ragtime, blues, swing, be bop, and avant garde, all those different voices of jazz—she was there listening, experimenting, playing, translating, arranging, composing. Above all, innovating. Sometimes her sounds were 'way up there ahead, but not so far that someone didn't hear.

Duke Ellington, with whom she traveled and arranged for a time in the 1940s, wrote in his autobiography, *Music is my Mistress:* "Mary Lou Williams is perpetually contemporary. Her writing and performing are and have always been just a little ahead throughout her career. . . . Her music retains and maintains . . . a standard of quality that is timeless. She is like soul on soul."

For me, her music takes me on journeys I'm not always sure I want to take. Her blues sometimes are *so* bad, so painful, I can't believe human beings can bear so much pain. But at the other end are her Masses—spiritual music so glorious, so full of love and joy, you wonder how one human being can stand so much *good* because you know there's an end to it.

When her "Mary Lou's Mass" was performed at St. Patrick's Cathedral in 1975, John Donohue, S.J., wrote in *America* magazine:

> On that afternoon, as on every afternoon, somewhere around the globe the nuclear submarines of the two superpowers were keeping their terrible vigils in the lightless ocean depths. But when the choirs, after the Communion, sang the Gloria of "Mary Lou's Mass," a hymn brimming over with joyful adoration, it was possible to believe, if only for the space of a shimmering moment, that true peace can be established among the nations.

Three thousand five hundred people *applauded* during that Mass. See how she connects? And all through her life of music, she has been connecting. Now she is at Duke University, in Durham, North Carolina, an artist-in-residence for the past five years, bringing jazz, the sound of soul, to a generation of kids who think music is rock and roll.

That's the good news. The bad news is that Mary Lou is not well. She is fighting a bad fight, but her music making hasn't stopped. She asked us not to forego our visit to Durham. She wanted to talk about her work and would we mind coming to the hospital?

This, then, is the account of a two day visit with her, off and on. It was an extraordinary experience, not only because of our talks. It was seeing Mary Lou and her music work magic on people from the unlikely confines of a hospital room. Would you believe nurses dancing down the hall, literally shimmying past her room where the good sounds were coming from a tape recorder? Would you believe patients, who didn't look as though they could walk, hobbling down the hall, intravenous apparatus in tow, to hear and get a peek at the lady who was making music?

And all the while an endless stream of visitors came quietly by—priests, nurses, her students at Duke, and always her manager, right hand, confidant, and friendly tormentor, Jesuit priest Father Peter O'Brien.

She is elegant, I realize, bending over her to shake hands, even with the indignity of intravenous. She wears a beautiful print gown, with gold chains around her neck, and spread on the bed are sheets of music for her new symphonic work, "The History of Jazz," which she is composing for the Duke Woodwind Symphony.

Before we begin to talk, she makes sure that Father O'Brien has brought along the rehearsal tapes from the first symphony session. She wants to listen to them later and make some changes.

"I'm doing a history of jazz, which will include all the eras of it—spirituals, ragtime, Kansas City swing, and bop, which I call the Dizzy Gillespie era.

"This is the introduction that I'm working on now."

I ask her how she can compose without her piano. She laughs a great roll of laughter, a sound I will grow to know well.

"I have finished this in my *head* already. All I need to do is remember what I've been humming. If it fits, it's *in*. If it doesn't fit, I have to take something out.

"I don't know what's going to come. I may write something down and it's the wrong sound. So I have to erase and start over again."

But how do you know it's the wrong sound, I ask, thinking again of no piano.

She smiles. "Because I play it over. Like I made a mistake here, you see, and when I came back from Mass, I looked at it and corrected it."

Finally, the light dawns. You play it in your head then. It's all *inside*.

"You got it. I hear it in my head. Like you hear words, I hear music."

She laughs at my incredulity. It is true I sometimes hear words in my head and sometimes can work out paragraphs mentally before putting them on paper. Why does it seem so hard for me to understand that she hears notes?

I ask if she feels compelled to write music.

"Do I have to? No, I don't have to. But I'd much rather. Or is what you mean, 'Do I walk around half-crazy with music going through the brain?'"

Yes.

"You're right. And then I get rid of that until the next thing comes along.

"I never wonder about how it is that I can hear music. And I never asked anyone. I just know that I *do*. I've been around several composers, but they never explained to me what happened to them. A couple were like me, like Duke Ellington. He would get an idea, and he'd lock himself into a room, and he'd stay there until he got it, you know?"

Mary Lou wrote once about jazz and the role of the soul in it: "From suffering came the spirituals. Songs of joy and songs of sorrow. The main origin of American jazz is a *spiritual*. Because of the deeply religious background of the Black American he was able to mix this strong influence with rhythms that reach deep enough into the inner self to give expression to outcries of censored joy which became known as jazz."

The creative process of playing jazz—improvisation—cannot be easily explained.

"The moment a soloist's hand touches his instrument, ideas start to flow from the mind, through the heart, and out the fingertips. Or at least that's the way it should be. Therefore, if the mind stops, there are no ideas—just mechanical patterns. If the heart doesn't fulfill its role, there will be very little feeling or none at all."

To Mary Lou, jazz played without love is not jazz.

Today she adds, "You know, jazz is 'way beyond the classics. People have been supporting the classics for centuries, but jazz is *your* music, created right here in America. It's the only true art in the world, because it came out of suffering of a whole tribe of people, not one. Our entire race. That's what makes it important.

"Americans don't realize it. At Duke University, they're beginning to. They didn't know anything about jazz before, but since I've been here, they're coming in. My students are not like the average kids. The blacks are much different. They are not hating. My black kids are smiling, and they're happy.

"When Frank Tirro (former chairman of the Duke University Department of Music) wanted to book me here, I was reluctant because I felt I should stay out and play jazz and be heard. But this is the best thing that could have happened to it."

Were you apprehensive about introducing jazz to a college class who were raised on rock and roll?

That roll of laughter booms out.

"It didn't matter because I was going to hook 'em anyway. I wasn't going to give up if I had to take them on, one by one.

"That first day in class I did my speil, then Peter played some old-fashioned blues, Billie Holiday, Bessie Smith, up until the present time, you know. It *worked*. The first day we had about thirty-three, the next day, we had some sixty-odd, the next day we had to move down to the auditorium."

Last semester, seven hundred had wanted to sign up for classes that had places for only one hundred and fifty.

"Usually you have kids squirming and leaving, but mine sit with their hands crossed and *listen*. And there's so much love when they leave, they go out laughing. One of the girls told me 'We should start a club and call it the Love Bond.'"

For the most part, jazz has been a love bond between Mary Lou Williams and her fellow musicians. Oh, there have been bad times, when she played music without the heart and heard jazz played without the heart, and we will discuss those. But when she looks back, most of the years were good, starting at the very beginning.

Her beginnings in music go back to when we see her mother drop her and run for the neighbors to come hear. From that day, Mary Lou learned to play the piano herself, spending hours alone, working out the sounds. Her mother never allowed her to take a formal piano lesson, fearing Mary Lou would lose her ability to play by ear.

It was the best thing she could do for her daughter. That, and invite the best pianists she could find to come to the house where Mary Lou could hear them play and learn from them.

When she was six, her family moved from Atlanta to Pittsburgh and settled into a neighborhood that was "biased." The new black family was welcomed with bricks thrown through the windows. The bricks stopped after a while. Mary Lou was quietly visiting the neighbors, playing the piano for them.

"I was never in the house. Once when I broke my arm, the neighbors came to the house asking for the 'little piano girl.' And my mother said, 'What have you been doing?' I said, 'Playing the piano at their house.'"

She roars, remembering her mother's astonishment.

In school, a teacher discovered she had perfect pitch, and the school principal took her to the University of Pittsburgh, where she played for professors and students. Word soon spread about the young prodigy.

"There was a music store in Pittsburgh. They sent instruments out to the house. My mother saw I began playing the violin. I just picked it up and started playing the 'Sheik of Araby' on it. So she sent me to a teacher for the violin. The teacher sent me back home and told her to leave me alone and that I would learn how to play myself. I was too far advanced. My mother should allow me to develop and go ahead and do what I was doing on the violin. But I never did like it. I was around seven or eight."

I had read that she played the piano for wealthy families like the Andrew Mellons, for parties.

"*Sure* it happened. The chauffeur used to pick me up in a limousine. There was a Mellon aunt, and I would go play the piano while she played cards with her friends. And she'd pay me. And I played for the Mellon boys who had a party going. When I got home, I'd have more than my stepfather made all week long." Once there was a check for $100.

What about your mother in your life? Did she encourage you to be a musician?

"I was alone, and nobody knew I was around. That's the type of family I was in. Somebody would come up on the porch and say, 'May I listen to your little girl play?' And she would say, 'Yes, come into the house.' That's *all*.

"Nobody encouraged me but my brother-in-law, Hugh Floyd, and especially Fletcher Burley, my stepfather."

At the mention of Fletcher's name, she smiles broadly.

"I *loved* that man."

It was Fletcher who took her to the theatre to hear good music. "Fletcher and Hugh always took care of me, especially if there was a new show. In Pittsburgh, anything musical happened, they'd take me to see it. To expose me."

It was at a theatre in Pittsburgh where she first saw pianist Lovie Austin. Lovie made an impression on Mary Lou that lasted for life.

"I was just a little kid. But I watched Lovie sit at the piano, play with her left hand, conduct with her head, and write music with her right hand. I copied her later on. That's how *I* used to do most of my arrangements, playing with my left, writing with my right. It's a wonder I'm not crazy."

From Fletcher, Mary Lou learned what she thinks is the most beautiful blues ballad ever written—"My Mama Pinned a Rose on Me"—and also a rollicking ragtime tune—"Who Stole the Lock off the Henhouse Door?" Both themes would appear years later, transformed under Mary Lou's touch but still recognizable in her "History of Jazz."

She starts to sing the words: "I'm gonna leave this hard luck town, I'm gonna leave before the sun goes down. Everybody's talking about the way I do...."

I ask her why that blues song is the most beautiful.

"You have to get your *own* thinking going in order to complete it. The writer doesn't tell what's going to come, but you *know*, anyway. That's what makes it the blues.

Earlier she wrote:

At one time in my career, I felt that the blues or boogie woogie were kindergarten music, a style of music that I should be ashamed of. But then I made the great discovery that all the eras in the history of jazz ... were based on the blues and the blues-feeling.... Now if I'm having difficulty getting the right feeling flowing as I play a set of music, I'll return to the blues straight ahead for one tune, then go back to my other music with more feeling. The blues is really the healing force in all forms of jazz.

Fletcher lived to see Mary Lou make it big, but he didn't approve of the new jazz she played in the 1940s, be bop.

"See, he was a boogie-woogie and blues man, and when I began to play other types of music he'd say, 'You can't play any more. I'm sorry, you don't play at all.' He was *blues*." She smiles sadly. "I don't blame him."

When Mary Lou was twelve, she went out on her first job, playing piano with a union band. When afterwards they weren't paid (a common occurrence in those days), she and the band walked the fifteen miles back to Pittsburgh. One summer she filled in for a pianist with a vaudeville troupe that played the carnivals. Those were real "animal" people, she recalls with a grin. A friend went along to chaperone.

How did your mother feel about you touring so young?

"She loved it, as long as I was with somebody. Had protection. But I've had freedom all my life, you know. I think it's good for kids."

She joined another vaudeville troupe when the headliners, a black husband and wife team, "Seymour and Jeannette," lost their regular pianist. Also in the troupe was John Williams, a saxophonist, and he and Mary Lou married, when she was about sixteen.

In the 1920s, vaudeville was a series of one nighters, touring all over the country, one small town after another. Wasn't that a hard life for a young girl?

She laughs. "I didn't even know I was touring. I was just having a ball, playing the piano. The *best* time of my life."

When Seymour died, the troupe went up to New York. It was about 1926. That was the first time Mary Lou heard Fats Waller play the piano and vice versa. When Mary Lou played for Fats, he was so tickled he threw her up in the air, all ninety pounds of her. A few years later, she would be sitting in with him on jam sessions.

Then John Williams formed his own group, The Syncopators, and they toured around the Midwest until John abruptly decided to join the Andy Kirk band in Kansas City.

"They offered him a nice salary so he went, leaving me in charge of the band in Memphis. Just a little girl, the leader of a band. I was sixteen." She shakes her head, thinking about that little girl.

I ask how she felt alone and in charge.

"No different. I think I'm a born leader. I just felt as if I were doing a job."

It was quite a group. Jimmie Lunceford, who would soon have a big band of his own came to replace John, Glen Gray, and Casa Lomas were some of the sidemen. She laughs, remembering one gig in Mississippi.

"After we finished playing, the man who hired us, one of those tough gangsters, said, 'I'm not going to pay you. I can get all the musicians I want, $2 a dozen. Jimmie [Lunceford] and the others got in the car and ran back to Memphis. *Left* me!

"I yelled, 'I want my money, I want my money, I WANT MY MONEY!' The man's mother and wife stuck their heads out the window and said, 'Little girl, go on, run.' Wife said, 'Look at my eyes, he beat me up.' But I said, 'I WANT MY MONEY!' I carried on so until he threw it down and said 'Somebody take her back to Memphis.' It was $15 for each musician, and I got their money, too!

"That man was evil, but he was going to have to kill me, and he didn't want to kill a woman. That was funny, 'I want my money, I want my money, I WANT MY MONEY,'" she yells, remembering.

A nurse peeks in, worried. We wave her away, laughing.

"Later I'd think about him and just *shiver* in the bed. There were a lot of those gambling places all through the South. Those cats were *tough*."

I ask her if there were times when she starved, because I had read that and wondered if it were true.

"I was with the Andy Kirk band then."

Was it really so bad that you weren't eating?

"It didn't *bother* me. I didn't feel hungry, because I tell you, we'd jam. Music is so great, when you jam, you wouldn't even get hungry.

"Once in Greeley, Colorado, we were playing but the man couldn't afford to pay us because nobody was coming in. That was during the '29 crash." They did eat corn right out of the cornfields then. But even that wasn't discouraging.

"I was too young. Everybody would laugh. If Andy came backstage afterwards with his head down, we knew he hadn't been paid. Then the trumpet player would blow 'Worried Blues' on his horn, and we'd all laugh."

Mary Lou made a little money by giving manicures to the boys in the band at five cents each.

Those years with Andy Kirk's Clouds of Joy were probably the most important years for Mary Lou Williams. Here she learned how to write music down and began composing her own pieces and arranging others. It was Kirk who taught her to write down the sounds that were dancing in her head.

"He would come in every morning at 11:00. I had great ideas that I told him about, and he'd take the ideas back to the band, but I couldn't write them down. So I began to watch and see what he was doing. He came in one day, and I had written an arrangement, but the tenor and the baritone parts were out. That's the only part I missed. And he showed me how to do that, and from that day on, I began to write myself."

She chuckles. "He just sat there too long with me." What happened was what she learned from him, she put to her own use and soon surpassed her teacher.

The buoyant music of the period was called Kansas City swing, a strong, blues-based kind of jazz that was being played not only by smaller bands like Andy Kirk but also by the Big Bands—the Dorsey Brothers, Benny Goodman, Jimmie Lunceford, Count Basie. And the music was played with love. Mary Lou wrote:

There was much love and charity among musicians in Kansas City. To develop new techniques and ideas, younger musicians listened to older musicians. All were very dedicated and devoted. Famous musicians from all over the world came to Kansas City to sit in on jam sessions to find to their surprise they had tackled such giants as Lester Young, Joe Jones, Count Basie, Ben Webster on tenor, Herschel Evans on tenor, Charlie Parker on alto. [Parker was a high school student then.]

She adds, "During this great swing period a pianist had to have two strong hands, especially a good swinging left hand, to compete as a top pianist."

That Mary Lou worked on, and she is one of the few jazz pianists in the business with two strong hands. Her left may be even stronger than her right.

I ask her if somebody told her to work on her left, or did she do it naturally?

"I'll tell you what happened. I was around *men*. People like Jelly Roll Morton, Earl Hines, J. P. Johnson, Fats Waller, and naturally I'm going to try to play like them. That's why I developed. And then they'd show me some different things I was doing wrong, and I'd end up on jam sessions, playing with them. All of them helped me. Art Tatum would tell you what to do. He wouldn't *show* you what to do; you had to learn what to do yourself.

"Tatum inspired me. Earl Hines. Fats Waller. J. P. Johnson. Art Tatum's music used to really get to me," she adds.

"But you know, I'm not that crazy about technique. I'm crazy about technique if it's original, like Tatum. Technique can be worse than rock on music. It can ruin it. But there's another kind of technique that you can be born with." Did I know what she was talking about? I knew.

She was not only arranging for Kirk, she began writing her own music. The first piece was a "little thing called Mesa Stomp." She wrote "Little Joe from Chicago" for Kirk, the first big band boogie-woogie music. She says frequently she is *not* a boogie-woogie artist, but she'll tell you she was trained to play *everything*, so she learned it and played it and wrote its music.

She wrote "Walkin' and Swingin'," which musicians love for the unusual voicing in the arrangement, "Steppin' Pretty," "Bearcat Shuffle," "In the Land of Oo Bla Dee"—over three hundred and fifty compositions. She tells how "What's Your Story, Morning Glory," a big hit, came about.

"That happened through a letter to one of Jimmie Lunceford's musicians Paul Webster. We used to write with music notes, in letters. So he wrote this tune, 'What's Your Story, Morning Glory? I haven't received a letter from you.' I wrote the music, had a guy do lyrics, and that's how it happened."

Jimmie Lunceford's band recorded it, and it became his forever.

Mary Lou began doing a lot of composing and arranging, not only for Kirk but the Big Bands. Benny Goodman ("Roll 'Em" and "Camel Hop"), Louis Armstrong, the Dorseys, and Duke Ellington were wiring her with requests for arrangements.

About her arrangements, jazz critic Whitney Balliett wrote in *The New Yorker*:

[They] were uncluttered and advanced. She used clarinet trios to spell out her attractive blues melodies; she opened and closed numbers simply with a soloist and the rhythm section; her improvised-sounding saxophone passages suggested the creamy writing of Benny Carter; and there were odd, beautifully constructed background harmonies, often played by the saxophones and trombones. Her best arrangements had a small-band compactness. They also had an almost schoolmarm purpose, and unfailingly pointed up both the tunes and the frequent solos.

The jam sessions she loves so tested a musician's solo inventiveness, and there were joyful confrontations as musicians took each other on, to see if they could outdo each other. She remembers one session in Kansas City when she was aroused in the middle of the night by pebbles on her window to go down and jam. Coleman Hawkins was downtown in his undershirt sweating and struggling for his life against Lester Young and Herschel Evans, and they had run out of piano players.

Another time she remembers stopping by a session after work, and they were playing "Sweet Georgia Brown." She went home, had a bath, changed her dress, and went back downtown about an hour and a half later. They were still on "Georgia Brown."

She was still in her 'teens. I ask how she felt sitting in on sessions with some of these fabulous musicians.

"They'd ask me to sit in with Fats Waller or Tatum, and I'd get nervous. I'd cry. I'd *cry*. Yeah." A soft giggle. "Somebody would say they were going to make a black eye for me. I should get up and *play*. If not, I'd be in trouble."

She drifts away, remembering. "A couple of the guys in the band would tell me, if you're in a session with Tatum, don't try to play the way he's playing. Play *your* style, play it well, and it will be accepted too."

She'd cry, too, over her arrangements and often wanted to work on them more than the musicians would.

"I'll tell you what happened a lot of times with Benny Goodman or somebody I was writing for. I'd done an arrangement for him, and I didn't like it, but they hadn't said anything yet. But I'd say, 'Hey, Benny, let me take that home and redo it, because I was sleepy last night.' That happened a *lot* of times.

"Duke Ellington once said, 'Oh come on, Lou, let us play it first.' And they played it, and it would be alright. You see, you can't get the feeling 'til they play it. I always wanted to pick up arrangements that I didn't like. 'Little Joe from Chicago' I picked up, and Andy Kirk made me pass it back. Then I found out it was a good arrangement."

What did you think was the matter with it?

"I rehearsed the saxophone section. And it was sounding funny. Then I rehearsed another section (and she sings out the beat), and I said, '*What?*' Everybody started laughing. And I said, 'Well, pass it in.' But they wouldn't pass it in, and I started stompin' my foot, crying, and I went to bed! They had to come to the room and get me.

"See, if you rehearse different sections like the saxophone and the trumpet separately, you get some funny sounds at times. But I found out those funny sounds going on fitted in with the trumpets. I found out it was *good*."

Did you ever have times when you couldn't do what you had in mind? That you felt you had failed at what you tried?

"Of course I didn't accept failure. I worked on it until it got alright. No, I never felt like I wanted to stop. I might rest a while and then come back if I got hung up on something. Or skip that bar. But then I'd pick it up again, do something about it. Then if it was still no good, I'd take it to some friend of mine, a composer, and say, 'Hey what's wrong with this?'"

Can you compose if you're upset or angry?

"Sometimes it will help me get straight. I've noticed something. If you try, you may do your best work then. Just try. You know?"

In the late 1930s, Mary Lou Williams married Harold "Shorty" Baker, Duke Ellington's first trumpeter. Both of her marriages were, for her, short lived. She said once in an interview with *Ebony* magazine: "I didn't marry men. I married horns. After about two weeks of marriage, I was ready to get up and write some music. I was in love with Ben Webster (the late tenor saxophonist) longer than anybody and that was about a month."

I ask if she ever regretted not having any children.

She looks surprised. "You know, I never even thought about it. I was so busy, I didn't have a chance to think about it."

In 1941, Mary Lou Williams left the Kirk band. Small things had been bothering her—untuned pianos and some new people he had hired who didn't set right. She abruptly left one night in Washington, D. C., and went home to her mother. She thought briefly about giving up music, but then traveled with the

Duke Ellington band for about six months, doing some fifteen or twenty arrangements for him.

One of these was "Trumpet No End," a dazzling arrangement of *Blue Skies* with the melody line completely hidden, to showcase the fabulous Ellington trumpet section.

In late 1941, Mary Lou Williams settled in on a long engagement at Barney Josephson's club Café Society Downtown, and it was an intense, creative time for jazz and for her.

Though the new jazz had roots in Kansas City swing, it also had new chords, different phrasing, a style and an approach to new places. Mary Lou was liking the sounds more and more. Even back in Kansas City in the jam sessions, musicians often asked her to play "Zombie" for them, and she would oblige with tantalizing 'outre' chords, new 'out' harmonies based on 'off' sounds. She wrote:

A new era of music called Be Bop came about during the early forties. Most of the musicians were my friends and they often visited my apartment to write or play their ideas. I loved them. They were more or less like the Kansas City musicians. So much love flowing from them. I learned a great deal about their chord changes and style of expression. The old blues took on a new look. The bop era blues chords added a great richness and more technique to jazz.

She told Whitney Balliett later,

All during this time, my house was kind of a headquarters for young musicians. I'd even leave the door open for them if I was out. Tadd Dameron would come to write when he was out of inspiration, and (Thelonious) Monk did several of his pieces there. Bud Powell's brother Richie, who also played piano, learned how to improvise at my house. And everybody came or called for advice.

Charlie Parker would ask what did I think about him putting a group with strings together, or Miles Davis would ask about his group with the tuba, the one that had John Lewis and Gerry Mulligan and Max Roach and J. J. Johnson in it. It was still like the thirties—musicians helped each other and didn't think of themselves.

Most of the musicians of the swing era didn't change, but Mary Lou did. She learned from the boppers: "Bop sent everybody back to school." They played all the time. When they weren't meeting at Mary Lou's, they were jamming at Minton's Playhouse in upper Manhattan or working in some of the many jazz clubs along 52nd Street.

It was in the 1940s that she began cutting a lot of records for Moses Asch's Folkways Records. She had previously cut a few with the Kirk band, and there are a couple of collector's items from her days with The Syncopators, but in the 1940's she recorded a lot of music with the bop musicians with whom she was sharing so much new sound.

Moe Asch, son of the famous novelist Sholem Asch, is unique among record producers. His first aim, above everything, was to get the sounds he loved on record, and he especially loved and cherished folk music of all nations. It was his style and his method of operation that attracted Mary Lou to him. He never interfered in the recording sessions. Mary Lou reports that he would "turn on the tapes, go downstairs, and leave us alone." No producer, no A&R man hovered around, getting in the way of the music.

In 1944 alone, Mary Lou recorded twenty-five sides for Moe Asch, and it is some of the freshest, most spontaneous jazz ever recorded.

Another reason Mary Lou liked Moe was contracts.

"I don't like 'em. They make you sign up to do a lot of things you don't want to do and that aren't good." She didn't want to be tied down, playing the same kind of music all the time, and Moe Asch didn't ask that Mary Lou sign a contract with Folkways. "He just gave me a lot of recordings to do for a year, and I went in and recorded."

Right there may be two of the reasons Mary Lou Williams is not a household name, except among jazz buffs. She refused to stay in a box, making the same kind of music over and over. And she would not sign a long-term contract with a record company that would, no doubt, promote her, but that would just as certainly keep her in a slot. She had been around long enough to know that businessmen, including record companies, are not comfortable with innovation and experimentation, and that's what she was doing during the 1940s.

Not only was Fletcher Burley upset with her playing, so were some of her old friends from the Kansas City era. That didn't faze her. She kept right on writing the new music, the new sounds she was hearing.

In 1945, she composed her "Zodiac Suite," twelve pieces based on the astrological signs. She wrote down three of the pieces—"Aquarius," "Scorpio," and "Pisces"—and planned to introduce the others on her Saturday afternoon radio program. As usual, she was busy; so instead of writing the rest of the suite in her head and then on paper, she composed it as she played it on her show. Each week, a new piece.

It was a major work, and several of the pieces showed the kind of musical innovation she was pursuing. I ask how the Suite came to be performed by the New York Philharmonic.

That great laugh rolls out.

"I'll tell you that story. Norman Granz asked me to play a concert for him. We used to argue like mad. So I said, 'I'll play a concert for you for *nothing*, if you get me with the Philharmonic.' And the fool *did*, the next day!" She roars with laughter. "I tell you, I was really shaking. You talk about being scared! I was shaking in my boots. I'd never written anything for a symphony before in my life. We had done "Zodiac" in concert, but that was with eighteen pieces. This was for a hundred. So I called my friend Milt Orent, who was very good. [He was an arranger and bassist on the NBC Network Orchestra.]

"Milt was so far out, they finally fired him. If he had to do a score for Kate Smith, he'd have the wildest things going on. He was about thirty years ahead in sound, he knew so much about chords and modern harmony.

"I said, 'Milton, you'll have to help me *do* this.' Milton worked on two of the pieces, then he had to go to work. So that left me with another tune and the boogie to score."

I ask her how she was feeling inside.

"I got all right the minute I started working; but I had to write and copy for a *hundred pieces*! I started at 7 o'clock at night and worked all night and went in at 1:00 the next afternoon. I passed out the 'Zodiac Suite,' second part, third. Then somebody called the conductor to the phone, and while she was gone, I said, 'Give me that one back, take this.' It was the boogie. The symphony had never played a boogie or anything before. Very biased about it too," she adds, grinning.

"I had been afraid to pass out the boogie while she was there." Another great whoop of laughter. "And so we started playing. When she came back, we were swingin'. You'd have thought Count Basie was on. I had thirty-six violins stand up and play like Charlie Parker." She does some scat music, imitating the sounds of the violins, and we both gasp, laughing. It hurts her to laugh, but oh, it feels good.

"So," she says, wiping her eyes, "when the conductor came back, she said, 'I've never heard anything like this.' It was a woman, I can't remember her name."

Billed as the first time jazz met the symphony, the concert at Carnegie was a smash, especially the boogie violins. And then "Zodiac Suite," lay dormant for eleven years, until Mary Lou performed it with Dizzy Gillespie's Big Band at the Newport Jazz Festival of 1957.

There were some changes coming in jazz and in Mary Lou's life.

All through the late 1940's, Mary Lou continued playing. She left Café Society, but worked in many of the jazz clubs along 52nd Street. In 1952, she went to Europe and stayed two years, but something was wrong. One night in Paris, she simply walked offstage and didn't go back.

"Walked out without my salary and everything. Nobody had done anything. Nothing especially had happened. I just stopped playing."

It was like the time in Washington, D. C., when she had abruptly stopped playing for Andy Kirk's band and went home to her mother. "Everybody was wondering why I did that. I do funny things at times. In Paris, I just walked off without notifying. I don't plan things like that. It's as though I might decide to leave this hospital. I'd just get up and start dressing." For an odd moment there, I think she's going to do it.

I ask her why she stopped. There were a lot of reports in the press that she felt jazz was evil. One magazine said she thought jazz was "the devil's own music" and that she could do nothing but pray for several years.

She shakes her head no. That wasn't it.

"Tired. I'd been working since I was a baby."

It was that simple.

And she's tired now. We've been talking enough and it's time to listen to the rehearsal tapes of the Duke Woodwind Symphony playing her new "History of Jazz." Do you want us to leave? I ask.

"NO!" And she turns on the tape.

The trumpets and clarinets sing out in a cacophony of sound that soon sorts itself into a haunting blues melody.

I like it. I'm smiling.

Mary Lou smiles, too, energy restored. "It's *wild*. But they got to *rehearse* it. Hear that part? They've got to pick it up!" she cries, snapping her fingers. "But they're doing good. This is their first time. This is the 'Introduction.' See, it's symphonic at the beginning, but it's going to go funky." She closes her eyes.

"There you go. Gospel!"

As the rhythms pour out into the hall, a little old lady patient comes by and says, "We're jealous. You got all the music in here!" Mary Lou smiles and keeps on snapping.

The music soars into the ragtime section, and things are really jumping now. A nurse shimmies past the door and repasses, shuffling, head back, hands waving.

The clarinets wail, and Mary Lou cries, "Mama, Mama, I don't know who stole the lock off the henhouse door?" The old lady leaves. A minister drops by to see her. Mary Lou turns off the tape to say hello.

"Ragtime," she explains, pointing to the tape recorder resting on her stomach, and turns it back on again.

"You look well," calls the minister over the music.

Again she turns the recorder off. "Makin' it," she says dreamily and turns it back on.

She frowns. "Playing the wrong beat on that!" She claps out the right one to show me. "That's what they do these days. Play the wrong beat." The young minister leaves, thinking hard.

"I like the blues myself," says George.

"Comin' up," says Mary Lou, and they do.

Milton Suggs, Mary Lou's bassist and the man directing the rehearsal in Mary Lou's absence, says on the tapes: "You can really get heavy handed on the last chords. Really bear down. Just express yourself within the bounds of what's happening."

Mary Lou listens critically. "Well, maybe it's the blues and maybe it isn't."

Were you satisfied with that?

"It's alright. But you see, you haven't heard it really. They're rehearsing, and you have to use your imagination on the rehearsal. The tempo has to be *faster!*"

We make a date for the next morning. As we leave, she's busy reading the sheet music and making corrections, intravenous still in place.

The next day, we resume talking about the years from 1954 to 1964, years when she was supposed to have given up music altogether.

"Oh, no. I've never gone that long without music. After I quit in Paris, for about six months I didn't play anything. I just rested. When Sarah Vaughan came over, we went on tour with Coleman Hawkins."

Then she returned to New York, but the sounds of jazz were souring for her. She was getting "bad vibes" from the owners of the places she played, from the people at the bars where she had to work, but worst of all was the bad sound she was hearing. Musicians weren't playing with love any longer. Jazz was cold. She began playing less and less; she began praying more.

Everyone talks about 1957, as though it was the time of a great religious conversion in her life, but from all she's been saying, I have the feeling she always had God in her life. I tell her that.

"You're psychic," she smiles. "I used to go up into my sister's attic and pray for hours. Nobody knew where I was or what I was doing."

In 1957, Mary Lou was received into the Catholic church. Soon afterward, she founded the Bel Canto Foundation to help musicians who were in trouble with alcohol and drugs. Bel Canto was not much different from what she had

been doing for years—listening to, helping, and talking with musicians. The difference was that now she was physically caring for the ones who needed help. She'd rent rooms for them, feed them, pray with them, help them get on their feet and get jobs.

She organized a thrift shop to raise funds for Bel Canto. Friends like Dizzy and Lorraine Gillespie, Louis Armstrong, Duke Ellington donated castoff, but expensive clothing. For several years, she maintained the thrift shop and lived on royalty checks from her records and arrangements. From time to time, when she needed money, she'd play a date, but that was rare.

Finally, her friend, Jesuit Father Anthony Woods, convinced Mary Lou she ought to return to music. "You're an artist," he told her. "You belong at the piano writing music. It's *my* business to help people through the church and your business to help people through music."

It dawned on her, too, that her music could raise more money for the Bel Canto foundation than the thrift shop could. She ultimately came to the conclusion that there was no reason why her religion and her music could not merge.

When another young Jesuit priest, Father Peter O'Brien, was drawn into her life by her music and became her enthusiastic manager, the merger seemed, to her, sanctioned from above.

In 1964, Mary Lou returned to a happy engagement at the Hickory House in New York, welcomed back after her self-imposed sabbatical by hundreds of happy jazz buffs. Also in 1964, Mary Lou wrote her first jazz hymn, a modern cantata in honor of the first black saint, St. Martin de Porres. When, in 1969, the Vatican commissioned her to write a Mass, it seemed at last that her music and her religion were irrevocably bound.

We talk about her music and playing it. When you are playing well and the music is coming easily, how are you feeling inside?

"Like I'm in heaven. You could cut my head off, and I wouldn't even feel it."

She once wrote about the "conversation" between instruments, when jazz is played the way it ought to be: "This feeling, the deep conversation and the mental telepathy going on between bass, drums and a number of other soloists are the permanent characteristics of good jazz. The conversation can be of any type: exciting, soulful, and even humorous debating."

Is there an instrument you prefer to work with, to make this conversation with?

"Just the bass and myself." She closes her eyes, hearing the sounds. "See, without a bass, you wouldn't have anything. You know the Spanish songs? If you didn't have"—and she claps out a tango rhythm—"you wouldn't have any rhythm or pattern at all. You have to have a bass."

But the bass can drive her crazy, too. Almost kill her with pain.

"I'll tell you why. You're so full of something that you're like this." Eyes closed, she pretends to play the piano. "Everything is going good and all of a sudden the bass will make a wrong note. It's like somebody *shooting* you. I remember reading once where a conductor dropped dead when one of his musicians had made a wrong note." There is a great hoot of laughter.

"You see, I won't be tense or anything because I'm relaxed and I'm grooving. The bass is still on earth, and I'm going some other place, and I don't think about the earth at all. I've had to leave him completely, and he's still down there and doesn't know what to do!" She grieves.

What then? Do you say anything to him?

"Sometimes." She giggles.

What?

"I can't tell you."

Why not?

"I call him a dirty name."

I'll put blanks in, I tell her.

"Put it down then. 'Get it on there, man,' I'll say. 'Come on, let's GO!' Someone said, 'Lou, didn't I hear you cuss over the mike?' I said, 'I didn't *cuss* over the mike. Maybe it *went* over the mike.'" She laughs.

So what did you call that bass player?

"S.B." She giggles.

A bass player's troubles once gave rise to one of Mary Lou's most brilliant pieces of improvisation. Father Peter O'Brien remembers it:

"A string on Milton Suggs' bass broke during a set at The Cookery in New York. Neither a replacement for the instrument nor a substitute bass player could be found. Mary Lou finished that set and two others, solo. The results were breathtaking. Everyone from Fats Waller to Monk to McCoy Tyner to the music of and beyond the spheres got into things that night. Her imagination was untrammeled and uninterfered with. She seemed to be bringing all of her powers of invention and all of her pianistic ability to bear that night."

We talk some more about improvisation, that magic time when a jazz musician outreaches himself and plays music beyond where he's ever gone before.

"You never know ahead of time if it's going to be good," she says. "You *hope.*"

She and Peter both remember the time at a private party when, playing for guests, Mary Lou climbed to that rarified atmosphere of true jazz. As often happens, there was no tape recorder present, and the sounds of that evening are recorded only in their memories. Mary Lou recalls that there was a very elegant woman sitting near Mary Lou as she played, a friend.

"This woman used to get so wound up when she drank, and wah, wah, wah, wah, she was in my left ear and getting on my nerves, and I didn't want to hurt her feelings. So I composed a tune from her voice. Later, I recorded it, and it was terrific at the recording session, but the one that night was *much heavier.* I called it 'The Scarlet Creeper.'" Mary Lou dissolves in laughter.

Do you feel nervous before you play? What about the times at the White House, the Carnegie Hall concert with Benny Goodman, or the one with the Philharmonic, or the Mass at St. Patrick's?

"You see, what I do if there's a big thing, like playing for the president, or the Mass, I put myself in another state and start maneuvering in that new place, over here. And I don't come back, or I'll get nervous. What I do is I hypnotize myself. At the Mass, I did go away into orbit. I don't even remember being up there. You know, I had a rehearsal before, and I forgot about it. I was in Saks, shopping for scarves."

The low laugh rolls out again. There is a huge impish streak in this woman, I've decided. She has secrets up her sleeve most of us haven't even thought of yet.

"When I got to the church, Father O'Brien was furious. I forgot the rehearsal! Oh, man!"

What about afterward? Is there a letdown being back on earth?

"Sometimes I feel embarrassed. Maybe I made a mistake. I was trained not to make mistakes. Sometimes the bass player could cause it, the drummer could cause it, maybe the audience. But in jazz we hate mistakes. We should play without mistakes."

Was there a point in your life when you felt that you had finally mastered the playing of the piano?

She looks at me in surprise. "You *never* feel that. You never get an ego with it like that. I never think of *me* doing this. It's God's music. I give Him credit for it.

"Nor would I ever say about something I've composed, 'This is my best work,' or give myself credit for it. No. You're getting into ego then, and you end up by not playing or writing anything after that.

"I'm not making music for Mary Lou Williams. I'm making music for people, for other people to enjoy, to love."

She sighs. "We need an awful lot of love today. A lot of people are making music without the love. That's why it's so cold.

"You know, I did some quiet research on jazz. I was wondering how it was I know so much. All of a sudden I said to myself, 'I was there each era, but I didn't realize it!' I went back through the years, and I said, doggone it, I was there in the '20s. I was in Kansas City in the '30s. In New York in the '40s. And I ran it down, and I realized I was there at the beginning of each era!

"And in each era, there was somebody there that helped me, and I didn't even ask them. Dizzy, Fats Waller, Andy Kirk, Monk, Bob Baron, John Williams. There was even one man when I was ten or twelve years old. I used to play with a bed sheet over the piano on those talent shows. I'd even play with my elbows, and just tear up that sheet. One time, a man was standing offstage when I came off. He said, 'Little girl, don't do that. I heard a couple of good things when you played. Stick to them.' I never played with a sheet over the piano again.

"This I'm sure of. I've never looked forward to anything else but music in my life, but as far as thinking it was my life to plan, I didn't. God had His hand in it."

Mary Lou Williams died on May 28, 1981.